QUOTES 1 - 100

1. It is not possible to will something to happen, but you can imagine it and be convinced inside that it is. If the world responds to your persistence, then you will have discovered the Lord as your wonderful human imagination.

2. You should explain the world to everyone you meet. This principle can be applied to anyone, regardless of their social or educational background. The ability to imagine creates reality.

3. Do not hold on to anything from the outside, but only hold on to your imagination. It is possible to lose something if you have assumed the loss of it at one point. . Take a moment to read more . Wondering what you would do if that were the case? Although you forgot about the thought, its message was already fulfilled. You must keep your possessions safe and not create barns for them.

4. Ancients realized that no instrument created by man could ever reveal the ultimate reality. To discover the ultimate reality, one would need to allow Mind to observe itself and then accurately record their observations. They concluded that any description of Mind that has been made by science could not be an accurate description of the Mind that made it. Today, we are talking about the ability to use imagination to see into the depths of the mind. It is also looking within itself. The goal of imagination is to observe oneself and to record these observations accurately. You will soon realize that imagination is the key figure in the Gospel.

5. It doesn't matter if it takes five hundred beings, both male and female to respond to your imaginal act. They will eventually come and appear to you to be the influence that makes your desire visible.6. Prayers cannot be made successfully if there is not a connection between the subconscious and conscious mind. It is possible to do this through faith and imagination. All men, imaginative and otherwise, can cast out enchantments in their imaginations, and all men, even unimaginative, are constantly under their control.

7. An example is the statement, "You must be born from above" in order to enter the Kingdom of Heaven. Although it is true in literal terms, the metaphor is used to illustrate the point. The young rich man asked: "How is it possible to enter my mothers womb again and be born again?" The womb is not higher than the rest. This is the birth of the second, spiritual man. From Genesis to the end, it states that God created everything and that he said "It is good." He repeats seven times: It is good. . The perfect number. You will one day see the entire world and say, "It is beautiful!" You will be able to animate it. Everything depends on what activity takes place in MAN. . It is important to spell the word in large letters as it refers to male-female garments.This generic God-man that you are is MAN, then you are MAN. All of the world is man-made. It is not a man, it is MAN. Even though all that you see seems to be outside, it is actually within your wonderful imagination, of which this vegetative realm is only a shadow. It can be difficult at this stage to believe that your world is a shadow. You are casting it and activating it.

8. If you believe that your imagination is Christ, and you want to be anywhere else, you can sleep there as if it were true. Don't let the fact that it is expensive or time-consuming stop you from dreaming. "I AM" infinite, and all yours and mine are mine. If Christ is your amazing human imagination, you can sleep as you wish. I don't know how it will happen, but you can ask me! Three weeks ago, a man called me and said: "Many years back in New York City, you told me that I could go to California if I believed I was there. My wife and I are now here, but I want to let you know that I am not convinced by what you teach. "I did what you said. But the reason I came to this place is because the company that I worked for opened a plant and transferred me there." He doesn't feel like he's flying through space. However, he was transferred by his company so he doesn't believe that feeling is the key!You take your pearls, and you toss them in front of the swine. They pick up your wisdom and drop it down. But you still throw it. Although you're warned not to do this, I can't discern who will accept it so I tell everyone who will listen.

9. "All that you see, even if it seems without it, is within. The world of death is only a shadow of it." If you can only imagine a state and believe it to be true, the outside world will follow your lead. It is your shadow that will forever bear witness to your inner imagination.

10. You are capable of believing. Although you may believe in stupid things, your belief and belief will make it happen. God, the one I refer to as God, is your stronger self but your slave for his purposes. He will wait on you just as quickly and indifferently when your will be evil as it is when it is good. He conjures images of good or evil as if they were real. He allows you to visualize whatever you want and projects it onto a screen so that you can experience it. It is so natural and easy to move into that you forget what moment it was planted. You also don't recognize your own harvest.

11. You are limiting your understanding of Jesus Christ to a tiny being. Jesus Christ is God's amazing human imagination. God created a state when you visualize it. Your world will then respond to your vision by fulfilling the role it has to.

12. Learn to pray. Learn it to make your world reflect the ideal you desire. Instead of thinking about, start thinking from. To see the wish fulfilled, you must stop thinking about it. If you place yourself in the state of the wish fulfilled, and you think from it, you're praying. In a way that your reasoning mind doesn't know, your wish becomes a reality in your world.If you can pray, you can become the man or woman that you desire to be. It is possible for anyone who believes. Learn how to believe and convince yourself that it is true. You will then be seen by another person who will call you or mail you a letter verifying your visit. This is what I have seen firsthand.

13.	Blake saw all human possibilities as "already made" states. He saw every aspect, plot, and drama as "mere possible" as long as they were not yet in existence, but as overwhelming realities once we are.

14.	If you believe that imagination can create reality, then test God. Is it really important what the rest of the world thinks if they actually try it? They won't believe the idea is crazy if they try it. They believed Einstein was insane. There are many who believe I am. It's okay, because God will eventually reveal himself to each person, and then the one who is Paul will be in the state of Saul. There is no other God because God took on all the human weaknesses and limitations of Man. God does not pretend to be you.He was your breath and had to accept your unique qualities. This was his crucifixion. Your body is the cross Christ wore, and no man was nailed to a cross bar. He is buried within you, and will rise from the grave. His tomb is his human skull, where he dreams. You sleeper, so awake! This moment may seem so real, but you are the reality of it and the central being in scripture.

15 You can demonstrate to yourself that your imagination can transcend what reason, eyes, and senses can tell you. This art is about daring to believe that you are more than your senses and reason would have you believe. Keep believing, and the world will change to the extent you can convince it. It is always conforming to your belief.

16.   The Bible is a testament to God's creative power from beginning to end. That same creative power can be used here in Caesar's world, as it is your amazing human imagination. Your dream will be fulfilled if you can conjure up a scene that would make it possible. Paul didn't expect the vision. It happened suddenly, almost like a great earthquake. It doesn't matter if you can conjure it, it just happens. You can conjure the scene that would fulfill your desires, but you must remain true to it in order for it to project onto the screen. It's something I have done countless times.Let's take a look at a simple scene. What if someone heard about your luck? Allow them to. Accept their congratulations as if they were actually there. Keep that vision in your mind. You can also listen to two people talking about your success if you need a more complicated scene. Listen to what they have to say about you and don't forget this vision. You can take the scene you have conjured up in your imagination with you. Its power is in what the scene implies.

17.   This art of revision will not only accomplish my entire objective but I also begin to revise it every day. It is my great purpose. I call it my amazing human imagination. When it awakens, it is the eye God uses to guide me into the world of thought. I now see that everything I once believed existed on the outside is actually within me.

18.   The words "God", "Lord" and "Lord", respectively, mean "I AM!" Awareness is the foundation of all life. The words God and Lord hide it like a mask. Instead of calling on the Lord's Name, call upon his name. You must use the word "I AM" to do this. Because all things are possible for God, you can call forth anything with his name. When consciousness is linked to desire, it can be called forth with God's name. You can call your desire for fame, wealth, health, or fame by saying: I AM rich, I AM famous, or I am healthy.If you do this, you will be calling God's name. We are instructed not to take God's name in vain. He will not hold us guilty if we do. If you say, "I am not wanted, I am nobody or I am no good," you have taken God's name and created exactly what He has assumed. . It doesn't matter if it is good or bad. You can make any assumption! You now know God's name. Trust in the true God, who is your amazing imagination!

19.   If man accepts the facts as conclusive, he will never use this God-given way of redemption.

20.   "Whatever you pray for, believe you have received it." This is the 11th chapter of Mark. "Whatever you want, believe you have received it." This is the First Epistle of John's 5th chapter, 15th verse. These statements are made by the Awakened Man. If the prayer does not get answered, it is likely that you are praying to the wrong god. If you realize that the God to whom you pray is your wonderful human imagination, then you can merely ask. It is the subjective appropriation or appropriation of objective hope. What is my objective hope then? It is subjectively taken by me. It is what I do. I just feel the fulfillment of my wish. It is mine. How would I see the world around me if it were true? Do everything necessary to make it look the way I see it. Let them see me as I would if I were a real external fact. If they and I are friends, and something in my life becomes public knowledge, . They would then know. Let them then see me as I would see them if it was true. The subjective appropriation is prayer. Don't ask anyone. Ask no one. It is your right to use it. You simply take it?

21.   I will tell you that when you awaken, you declare the supremacy of imagination and place all things under its control. Never again will you bow to the dictates and accept the world as it is. Truth is not limited by facts, but only by the intensity and creativity of your imagination.

22.   Know what you want and work towards it. It is now necessary to add faith, because without faith it will be impossible to please God. Imagine a state, and you will feel as if it is now a reality. Imagine it for free. In fact, you're imagining everything at once. Let me tell you, if you allow your imagination to create the desire, it will become so easy to believe it was your imagination that made it possible. If you do, you'll be back in bed.

23.   Everything is yours to use, not just what I said. This world is amazing because you can travel to unknown places by gondola, learn about animals, fruits, and birds that aren't found here, and you have complete control over your life. Man is completely unaware of what he is eating while walking on the earth. Anger, jealousy, hate and thoughts of horror, anger and hatred feed invisible monsters that cause pain and heartache. Some people want to eat the spoiled fruit that is part of this age. But once you enter that age, your power is unlimited. Everything is a thought that you can control.According to the Bible, "Eye hasn't seen, ear not heard, and it hasn't entered into the heart" of those who love God, the things God has prepared for them. You will find that you can be one with your Father when you become one with him. Set your eyes on the world that Christ will reveal to you. Each person will experience a unique awakening as they awaken one after another. However, the symbolism and time elements will still be present. Between the vision of God's birth and the revelation, it takes five months.

24.   Paul says that God can be found by seeing phenomena. "All of his invisible things are clearly visible from the beginning of all time." How? The things that are made. Did God not tell us: "I kill and make alive, I wound and I heal." I can do all things, and no one can deliver from my hands. This is not trueBeing on the outside speaking, but it is the imagination who is the Lord. There is no other God. Can't you just say "I AM"? That's He. Now that you have found God and are able to worship him, be a God. Honor your imagination as God when you see what you've imagined. You may see God as someone high up, but that is not how God works in your mind. While you know that you can do unlovely things, you cannot believe God could. Yet, I affirm God. . Your imagination is the limit. . capable of healing, making alive, killing, or wounding.

25.   Let someone who wants to be self-pityful indulge in it. You are not supposed to test the man, but you should. It is not your job to prove it to anyone else, but to yourself. The world is nothing but you pushing it out, and all of it is there to help you imagine the future. Your perception of the world will determine the behavior of the rest of the world. No matter how your personal life may be, the entire world is you pushing out. Everyone in it is there for your imagination to help birth all your fantasies. It doesn't matter if it takes one person or one hundred thousand. Everyone will do his part and you don't need to ask for his permission. Your world is animated by your amazing human imagination.

26.   This lecture was a reminder that almost everything in the world is not what it seems. This is not speculation. I'm not theorizing. You have the power to change your life. This power is not external. It's within you. You will learn how to harness it. Your imagination is what animates the world around you. Change your imagination and the world will change for you.It is impossible to try to change the circumstances without changing my own imaginal activities. I must fight against my very nature, which is what is animating my world. If I believe I am being hurt or that others are against my, then I have created them in my world. If I believe all are working for my good, then they must also work for my good. They don't have to ask me. They don't have to do it. It is something I do within myself. The whole world around me exists in me. It is me that "pushes it out". It is objectified. I don't need to change the situation; I can only make changes within myself. And then, everyone, even if I know him by name, is "pushed out."

27.   You should use your imagination to love everyone and believe in the reality of what you imagine. Listen carefully to your friend who is interested in a job. His hand will touch yours. You can see his smile. You can use every sense to create the scene. Keep going until you feel the excitement of reality. Then let it go and let the scene unfold on its own. According to the Bible, the kingdom of heaven looks like a mustard seed.The seed is what you have created in your imaginal act for your friend in heaven. It is not necessary to pick it up in order to check if it's growing. Leave it alone and it will continue to grow and blossom as a fact in your world. This will reveal the hidden cause of Christ within you. Christ, the power, wisdom, and eternal life of God is within you. As the Hebrews 13th chapter states, He will not leave you nor forsake your side. You might find yourself in a miserable situation and end up going to hell. But if this happens, you will know that there is someone who loves you and will never leave you.

28.   Here's what I discovered. My amazing human imagination is the Spirit God. You can enter any state of this world and it will transform into reality. It is reality. Why? Because you are the reality that dwells within it. Things are real wherever you are. They are real if you're not there. They return to their flat surfaces. All things are possible in the human imagination.The state where we will live is up to us. . The state we will be entering and making real in our world. It's all about feeling. If it were true, how would you feel? What would it feel like to experience this feeling? How would it change my perception of the world? Once I am in that state, I try to give it the tones and vividness of reality. It will work if I can give it sensory vividness, the tones, even if I don't see it. But sometimes, it becomes so vivid, so intense that you actually see it. It opens up. The whole thing becomes real when your eye opens. . The world you have always wanted is now possible because you are a part of it.

29.   President Hoover was born in poverty and rose to power in America. He said this at a San Francisco convention: "Human History, with its forms and governments, its revolutions and its wars, and in truth the rise or fall of nations could all be described in terms of the growth and fall ideas implanted within the mind of men." The 8th chapter of Nehemiah tells us that Ezra read the Book, the law of God, with interpretation so that the people understood what he was saying. My hope is that I can understand the meaning of the Epistle of John and President Hoover's words. These are the words: "I AM FROM above; you're from below." You are from this world, but I am not. "Now I tell you, unless I believe that He is God, you will die in sins." Sin is to miss the mark. So he says that unless your believe that you are already what you want to become, you will never achieve it. Would you like to feel secure? You can then say to yourself, and only you: "Unless my faith in me is secure, I will be condemned to eternal damnation." I will continue believing I am insecure, thereby missing my purpose in life." If you cannot believe that "I AM secure", even though there are no supporting facts, you will never feel secure. In the name of God, I AM, and there is no other. The source of imagination (I AM), is above. It is possible to imagine anything, even though imagination is not a part of the real world. This is the story of scripture.

30.   If you know what you want, you can assume that you have it. Be confident in your belief. Visualize your world mentally to see the fulfillment of your desires. This will help you to call forth a response from your thoughts and in the near future, you will be physically in the place you have imagined.

31.   Only one cause can explain the phenomenon of life. God is that cause. This is something I have seen firsthand. God is the only creator. His imagination works in your deepest soul. God started a good work within you, and He will complete it when God's creative power becomes visible in you. Scripture refers to God's wisdom and creative power as Christ. Christ will reveal himself to you and you will realize that you are God's power, God's wisdom. God, your amazing human imagination, is the source of all your faculties. It flows into your surface mind least disguised as creative, productive fantasy. If you think about what you can do in order to overcome your current limitations of life, then you are dwelling on the ends. God doesn't

ask you to think about the ends, but the means. God speaks to you through the medium called desire. He asks: "What do thou want of me?" He then tells you to forget about the means and methods, as his ways are impossible to search. They are beyond understanding and inexplicable. This is the 11th chapter of Romans. Don't worry about how God will accomplish the end. Only know that He will. Can you believe your desire is fulfilled? Is it possible to believe that it is true? It is possible to believe it, and you are free to take it.

32.   If you truly desire something, speak it and then act. It is possible to move from one place to another and not change. It is important to look within and see the world as the person you desire to be. You have already moved from where your desires were to the fulfillment of them. You can only imagine the motion. If the desire is true, no matter what the world does, you can stay in this state and bring it to light. However, it is impossible to transform an invisible state into an outer visible one without moving.Because everyone has the ability to imagine, it is possible for anyone to do it. God is God and everything is created by God. I am a believer in you. I have introduced to you the creator of your existence. You now know him, don't be like Paul the Roman, who was able to recognize God but did not revere him as God. He exchanged God's immortality for an image that resembled Him, and the true knowledge about God for a lie, serving the creature, rather than the creator, the imagination.

33.   There are many states. The state of health, state of sickness, state wealth, state poverty, state of known and unknown. . All states are just states, and everyone is always in one state. Each of us has a state that we love and return to time after time. This is our home. We can always escape from a state that isn't pleasant. This is how it works. All states are mental. It is impossible to escape your current state by pulling strings from the outside. To move towards the desired state you must mentally adjust your thoughts. Your current state was brought on by you, either intentionally or unwittingly. The state became living and grew, bearing the fruit you don't like. Its fruit could be poverty, distress, heartache or pain.There are many unlovely fruits. You

can still get rid of your unlovely harvest by changing your human imagination. What would you like to harvest? Once you have identified the feeling, you can ask yourself how it would feel if you could harvest your wish right now. Once you feel the feeling, it is easier to capture it. For me, it is easier to feel the feeling when I imagine I am with friends and that they see me as if my wish were a reality. When the reality feels real, I am able to fall asleep. In that moment, I am in a state.

Now I must make this state as natural and normal as my current state. I

I must be conscious of returning to my new state every day. It must feel natural, just like my bed at night. The new state is unnatural at first, much like a new suit or cap. Even though no one notices that your suit is brand new, you feel like everyone is watching you. Its fit and feel are all you notice until it feels right. Your new state is no different. It may seem strange at first, but you soon become comfortable with it. You will find that you can always return to it because it is natural to you.

Most of us know what we want and can create it in our mind's eye. But, we never actually occupy it. We don't move into a state to stay there. This is what I call perpetual construction or deferred occupation. Although I can dream of having a beautiful home, I will not be able to afford it. I may postpone my plans to occupy it until another day. My friend may have wished he had a better job. It may be something I imagined, but if I don't believe he is there, then I have only constructed it for him and not occupied it. I can imagine him or her being different all day. But if I don't go into the state to view him from it, then I don't occupy that state. He remains in an unloved state relative to me. This is the world we live in.

It is impossible to imagine a thing that isn't part of a state. However, the life of any state lies in the person who occupies it. Because God's name, "I AM," is the only way to give life to a state. It is not "You Are" or "They Are." God's eternal name, I AM, is it! This is the essence of the universe's existence. You must be there if you want to make a state live. You are happy when you're in a kind, gentle, loving state. This means you see others as beautiful, live graciously, and enjoy life to its fullest.

To make this state of being natural, you need to see everyone in your life as kind, gentle, and loving. While others may not see them that way, it doesn't matter what their opinions are. If I asked people what they think about me, I'm pretty certain that no one would agree. Some people would call me a deceiver while others consider me the closest thing to God. A person's state of mind when asked to describe me would determine if they are a devil or a God.

If you apply this principle and know it, you can achieve your goals. However, you are the operant power. It doesn't operate by itself. Although you may be able to know everything about the law, it is not enough. You must act on your knowledge. The operant power within you is "I AM". Your awareness should be at the center of what you desire. Keep at it until your desires are realized. Because there is a long time between the promise and the law, learn to use it.

34. The law of reversibility is a knowledge that enables the disciplined man to transform his world by only imagining and feeling what is beautiful and good. He will never fail to inspire others with the beautiful idea he has within him.

35.   Where did they go when you had a dream of many people tonight? They are all part of you, created and acted upon by you. Are you not a protean? All Imagination is God the dreamer. You imagine the many roles you play. You are part of a dream at this very moment. Others around you are playing their roles because you are imagining them. You are your spouse, your husband, your children, friends, and enemies. You are all of them, because there is only God (Imagination).

36.   It is not possible to say, "I am going to be rich." You must believe in yourself that you are rich by saying "I AM rich." Because God is active and creative, you must believe in the present. He is your awareness and God is the only one who acts and is. His name is forever and ever "I AM", therefore he cannot say "I will be rich" nor "I was rich", but "I AM rich!" You can claim what you need to know right now and. . Although your rational mind and senses may deny it, it is still true. . If you can feel it, your inward activity will be perpetuated and will be reflected in the outside world. . which is nothing but your imaginal activity objectified. It is futile to try to change the circumstances in your life without changing its imaginal activity.

37.   Your talent, which is your imagination, can be used now. You should use it every day. God will be pleased if you use your imagination. It doesn't take a lot of effort to imagine what you want. As you walk down the street, imagine what you can see. It's easy to make a simple assumption and it can be a lot of fun. Today, a friend called to thank me for helping her sell her house. The house was an immense one in Highland Park that had been vacant for a while. When a man approached the door, he asked to purchase the house. She had previously hired a woman to clean the house. The house was sold two weeks later. What was I to do? I imagined her telling me that the house had been sold. That was all I did. There was nothing more I could do. All things are possible with God and he loves me so much that he will honor any request I make.

38.   Mark tells the parable about the fig tree. . cursed. It was found to be withered to the roots. Awakened imagination called attention to this fact and said, "Have faith that God." Truly, I tell you, whoever said to this mountain, "Be taken up, and cast into the ocean," and doesn't doubt in his heart that he will see it through, it will happen for him. So ITell you that whatever you want, when you pray, believe that you have it, and you will." Mark 11.

This is an imagined act that has no support in reality. Although the cursed tree did not become wilted, the tree had already been cured by the time they returned to it the next day. This law does not limit itself to being only constructive. You can use it for good or bad purposes, or for indifferent ones. There are no restrictions on prayer's possibilities. When you pray, you should immerse yourself into the feeling of the desire fulfilled. The word "pray" is "Motion towards; Accession to; At or in the vicinity of." You can then point your gaze towards the fulfillment of your wish and accept it as reality. You can then go on your way, knowing that your desire is yours. It was possible and it will come to pass. You will be amazed when this happens the first time you practice it. But once you understand how to accept the assumed state, you will realize that you don't have to do anything to make it happen. The assumption has its own plan for fulfillment.

This world is only an illusion. . without any external object to support it truth. . When truth is maintained, it will become fact. This world is not essentially imagined if an imaginal act creates an external fact to support the idea. You can believe in it if you are willing to accept what your senses and reason deny. . If this happens, how can we know that the world is solid and real? You are God, and everything is possible. . All imagination! God is in you, and you are in Him. Even though you can't remember how or when it was created, the world is everything you imagine it to be.

39.	My experience taught me that I am supreme in my own circle of consciousness, and that the state I identify with determines how I experience it. It is important to share the truth that imagination creates reality. To know this, you will be free from the greatest tyranny in the world, the belief of a second cause. Blessed are those whose imaginations have been cleansed of second-hand beliefs. They know that imagination is all and all is imagination. Through a series mental transformations we become more aware of the existing creation and match our mental activity to it. We activate it, resurrect and give life to it.

40.	You should control your imagination. If you want to steer a course towards a specific goal in your life, you must always be aware of where you are heading. You can only know what you want when you believe it is within you. You can make it happen, and no power can stop it from appearing.

41.   If they were being honest, men you and I admire would admit to allowing their minds to be degraded and elevated. While many people know what they're doing, they don't know Christ. They would be able to see that we don't have to make us feel inferior to become better. You don't need to be a burden to others to achieve your goals. Your reality is that you are I AM. You can raise your consciousness, and you will rise. But you won't be able to lift another person down by saying "I am better than". Tonight, take this law and use it. It will work, I swear. As if you were speaking to another person, you can go into your wonderful human imagination when you go to sleep. While you know that you are thanking your imagination, you should also acknowledge your Father. You were born from the Father and entered the world. You are now leaving this world and heading to the Father. You will eventually reach him. There is no other Father. There is no other God!

42.   Tonight, when you go to sleep, just say "I AM." You can add any condition that you want to the I AM, and it will be true. As if you were speaking to God, imagine your imagination. He created and sustains the universe. Ask yourself who is creating it when you think of something. You will answer "I AM." This is God's name for all eternity. Visualize and dream. Be confident in believing that you can achieve anything with your amazing human I AMness. Try it! It doesn't matter if you are able to kneel and pray to someone on the outside. You don't have to cross your arms before any icon. The Lord is your imagination, your consciousness and your wonderful I AMness. God is the only one who can stop being. . He who is in your consciousness is he. . It was created in love.

43.   "I am the beginning and the ending. There is nothing that can't be done."It has not been and it is." Consider creation finished. . You and I are not the only selectors of what is. Selectors means that you and me have the privilege, but we may not use it. It is our privilege to choose that part of reality to which it will respond. In doing so, we create it for ourselves. We don't realize we are so fortunate. We just live in the world as it is, without realizing that we have the power and ability to change or out-picture the circumstances of our lives.

44.	Don't turn your back on someone who comes into your life. Instead, look at his desire as clay that you can mold into something. You can take the same person and make him into whatever state you choose. Rework him to become a man who is more productive and happy than he's ever been. This is all you need to do. It is not your concern how the funds will be used to support his employment. You only want to be the best potter. You were given the individual as a spoiled vessel. It is not to be thrown away, but it can be used to make another vessel. . The potter . to do.

45.	You will be able to control your imagination if you understand who you are. You will soon be their victim if you don't. If you use your imagination to help another person, you are doing the right thing. It isn't done in love, but that is where the question marks are. God is love. This knowledge is not based on philosophical reasoning but self-revelation. God revealed himself to me, and I now know that God is infinite love. He is also Infinite Wisdom and Power, but without love, it can cause horror. Believe me, I tell you. Your amazing human imagination is the Jehovah and Jesus of scripture. There is no other God and God is love. This truth will be revealed to you one day.

46.	The characters in scripture are therefore not historical. To see anyone. Jesus Christ. . As a human being who has walked the earth, it is to see truth with the weakness of your soul and to be unable to bear revelation. Jesus Christ is the ideal state in which you can move. In that state scripture unfolds to reveal who you are as God. Who is he? He is your amazing human imagination! All things are possible if you have an imagination! What would you do if God imagined that you were exactly what you desire to be? What would you think? What would you do? Do it. You can feel it becoming a reality. Your hope is in your desire. Your imaginal act represents your subjective appropriation and realization of the hope that you wish to attain. Faith is the link between God's power and your desires. He doesn't question your desire. He, who has all knowledge and creative power, just gives it to you. Christ is the power and wisdom of God.

47.   All the invisible things of him since the creation of the universe are clearly seen by the made things, so you will be able to recognize your harvest when they arrive in your world. It will be brought in by you, but it is not yours. . You are unaware of your actions and have traded the truth about God for a lie. How? You exchange the immortal God, which is your wonderful human imagination, in exchange for an image of a man. You believe that a man is responsible for bringing your desires to fruition. However, this is false. Don't believe that tonight you inherit a fortune because of the man who helped you to get it. No. You assumed wealth before that event. He was just an instrument, an actor who played his part in getting you the money. It could have been from someone completely unrelated. It doesn't take a grandpa, aunt, or uncle to make it happen.

48.   Your imagination is unlimited, except for what you put on yourself. You are only as limited as your financial, intellectual and social picture. You alone, and only you, have the power to expand your understanding of causality and plant or reap all that you desire. Your desires are like the sheep in your pasture, and your shepherd is your wonderful human imagination. Bring your dreams back to the fold if they have wandered. Tonight, read the 14th chapter from the Gospel of John. It is a beautiful chapter. It's the entire Bible. It is so thrilling to just read each verse. When they asked him to show the Father in this chapter, he replied: "I have been with them all these years, and yet you don't know the Father." You can see the Father when you see me. How can you then say, "Show me the Father?" He continues, "I dwell within you, and you dwell within me, we are one, and I AM the father." This is a difficult statement for man to grasp and it's not something you can blame. So, I say that the greatest need for human imagination is a fresh thinking. All the problems and conflicts of the world will

disappear if man can see his own imagination as Christ. When one sees himself as Christ, there will be no barriers.

49.   God, the Father of all things, is in you! Your truename is "I AM", and there is no other God. You will never be able to believe that "I AM He" is true. As there is no God (imagination) in the world, you must assume you are the man or woman you desire to be now.

50.   My words are not enough. I am God. Your desire can be called forth by calling God's name. Ask yourself what it would look like and how it would make you feel if it was true. Next, assume that you already have it. After you assume it, let the people you know now see you. You don't have to make them see you. Let them see the change. The world is a box that echos and reflects what you've assumed. Listen to what your friends have to say about your changes. You will see their expressions of happiness at your good fortune. As you continue to wear your current body of belief, feel that feeling. Keep wearing that feeling and your desire will become a reality in your life. You will then discover the true cause of all phenomena. Only one source exists. It is called God by the world. It is a beautiful name, but remember that God is your awareness! You cannot see me!

51.   Victor, Neville's brother, doesn't smoke or drink. But he sits alone in his room and continues his inner conversations about fulfilling his desires. He can control his imagination. He has complete control over his inner conversations and things will work as he intends. He doesn't go to church. He is a religious man, in the truest sense of the term. He is generous with his donations to charity. You wouldn't know how many people he helped in the Island, as he doesn't publish it. He has discovered that his inner conversations can help him achieve this.

52.   Paul says: "He loved and gave himself for your sake." Imagination became you in order to love you. This is Christ, the Christ. There has never been another Christ, and there will never be another. Try your imagination and find Christ. Do you really need someone to help you? Are you in need of an anti-poverty campaign to help you? What a difference it would make for those who are on relief to believe in Christ! They go to church instead and give it a portion from the relief they receive. They believe in emotionalism, but they don't know the source of all phenomena.People on relief believe their income comes from Uncle Sam, despite the fact that he doesn't exist. There is no government that has money! Before money can be given to anyone else, it must first be taken from you. The money we earn in this world is taken from us to be given to the Mr. Seeons. If it is not stopped, the so called government will be criticised for stopping the gift.

Except for not telling the truth about Christ, the churches haven't fallen apart.

Instead of giving to the poor, they should be telling them who Christ is! What does the world think if I tell you Christ is, and you test him? Does it matter what the world thinks if there is proof for something? This can be proven in performance. What does it matter what everyone else thinks? If you have the ability to test your imagination, and prove its creativity, then you don't need to ask any priest, rabbi or minister what they think!

53.   You can claim that you want to live in a beautiful home. Although you may think you cannot afford it, that is just an imaginary thought. Instead of dwelling on the possibility that you cannot afford it, I suggest that you accept the reality that you do have the money to buy it.

54.   Remember that God is you and creates and sustains the world through your imagination. There has never been another God, and there will never be one. Imagination is the only God.

55.   All successful operations are based on a persistent imagination that is centered in the fulfillment of the desire. Only this can help you achieve your goal. The conscious, voluntary use of the imagination is the key to every stage of man's development. You will then understand why poets stress the importance of vivid, controlled imagination. This is the William Blake version:"In your own body you bear your heavens and earth.

All you have to do is look, even if it seems without.

It's within you, in your imagination

This world of death is only a shadow.

It's easy to do, and it will be clear that your imagination is the creator.

56.   This is how it works. After each day is over, I look back at it. I don't judge the day. I just review it. I review the day. I go through all episodes and all meetings. Then, as soon as I have a clear picture of it in my mind's eye I revise it. It is rewritten and made to reflect the perfect day that I would have experienced. Scene after scene is rewritten, revised, and then I imagine that day. I then relive it in my imagination, revising it. This process continues until my imagined state takes on the qualities of reality. It feels real. I experienced it. I know from personal experience that the revised days can change my future.

57.   I will only accept or hear anything that contributes to the idea I hold about myself. For I will know that I am secure. A headline might be a shocker to the world, but I won't accept it. If I don't acknowledge it, it cannot proceed from me. All things are made manifest when they are admitted, but not unless they're admitted.

58.   It is like you strike a chord when you visualize something. Everything that responds to that chord bears witness to your activity. The world responds to your imagination. David, a man after my own heart, will do whatever you ask. . Is David not the outer universe? This is not "will", as the world uses it. It is not possible to will something to happen, but you can imagine it and be inwardly sure that it is. If the world responds to your persistence, you will find David.59. An imaginal act can be described as a creative act. The moment the seed (or state), is felt, it is fertilized. It may take some time for the seed to become a reality. So, start today by pretending you are the man or woman you want to be. Let your imagination guide you and the people around you. Keep your assumptions true. This thought is the key to bringing your desires to fruition. Do not persist in fear or effort, but rather wait for your imaginal act to become a reality.

60.   You don't have to think, even if you are innocent of the words, that they are an idle thought. Why? Because you are God and God's words can never return to him empty. They must achieve the purpose he set out and prosper in the task for which he sent it. Even though you don't know the Law, you can still operate that Law. You will still reap the rewards.

61.   Robert Frost, the late Robert Frost, said that "Our founding fathers didn't believe inthe future. They believed in the future." Your ability to believe in a thing is the most creative power you have. The passage of time did not produce the country our founding fathers desired. They wanted democracy and not a monarchy and they knew that waiting and hoping would not bring it about. . They had to take it home, so they believed it in. How? Faith. They subjectively ascribed their desires.

62.   One day, I was fired by J. C. Penney Co. I worked for J. C. Penney Co. for one year and a half, running their elevator, and being their errand man. My salary was $22. I made $5 per week and paid $5. I was unable to understand why they had let me go. My dreams and my desires transcended their position, so they had no choice but to do what was necessary to make my dreams come true. You are responsible for the manifestations in your life, I assure you. . It doesn't matter if it is good, bad, or indifferent. If you find the news distasteful, then you are the dreamer for that storm. The day will come when the storm will end. Awareness is the only cause. It is easier to offer advice and point out where the other person is wrong than to admit that he is only reflecting your mistakes. Although it can be difficult to accept that the world is witnessing your thoughts, it is true. Do not judge someone or something if you don't like it. Instead, look inside to see who is creating the image.

63.   You can believe that you have it if you believe in yourself. You can and will get help from many men, even if they don't know it. You don't have to convince others to help; all you have to do is believe that you are what it is you want and then let the world (which really is nothing but you pushing out) make that assumption. I promise you:Your desire will be fulfilled because all things are possible for those who believe.

64.   In the 14th chapter, John tells us: "Let your heart not be troubled, you believe God, believe also me. There are many mansions in my Father's house; would it not have been so that I went to prepare a place? "When I prepare a place, I will return to you and say to you that I AM there also." This may seem like a man speaking to a group, but it was the human imagination who spoke these words. . After being rescued by the Father, he gave his life for us. Human imagination has left the world and is returning to the Father's home. He returns to find the source, or cause, of all the phenomena that make up life. Jesus Christ, your amazing human imagination, is the key to all things in the world. . But specifically to the Father.We will be presenting this thought at a practical level tonight so that everyone can bring in whatever he wants into the world. Today, billions of dollars are spent on anti-poverty programmes. But the only thing that will truly consume us (and it won't cost one nickel) and is a new Christology. This new Christology allows us to see Christ as the source of all our imaginations. Christ is the cause for all things, but the churches continue to mislead people. . by teaching, he is outside as

someone who lived and died 2000-years ago. To whom you should pray and turn, . You will never find him. No matter how much money is distributed to the poor, poverty cannot be overcome from the outside. The only way to overcome poverty is to tell the poor that he is the source and teach him how to pray and turn to God. This is why it is so important to share the new Christology with everyone you meet. . It doesn't matter what you do. . You will never achieve your dreams.

65.   When I refer to imagination, I mean God in you. There are two sides to this coin: imagining or contacting. Imagine it as a contact. Imagine and you will contact a feeling. Your power is limited by the fact that you are not covered in flesh and blood, but God created all things. I hope you are able to understand the rules of the game of life. . Because there are positive and negative rules. . I implore you to not curse anyone. Ecclesiastes used "king" and the "rich" words because they were the most envied. To be envied, one does not have to be a millionaire. You could be just a bit more fortunate than the next person. To be envied, someone could live in a better area, pay more rent or even buy better clothes.We are told not to curse the rich or the king in our thoughts. They cannot be hidden, since all thoughts are one. As everyone outside is aware, awareness seems scattered. If he wants to change the world on the inside, he doesn't need to ask anyone else. He will ask another person if he is needed to effect the change. . With or without his permission. It doesn't matter who you choose to be the catalyst for the changes you envision. Because we all intertwine, he will do his part. You just need to stand at the end from within.

66.   You are the world and you can express your inner thoughts, your imagination.

67.   Jesus is your hope for glory. He is your amazing human imagination. As God's wisdom and power, imagination is the work of God until Christ is born in you. Your history will change from BC to AD on that day, and each year thereafter will be the Year of the Lord. Christ has been born in you. The words of Isaiah are now yours: "For you a child was born and a boy is given." Your government will then rest upon your shoulders. You will become the Wonderful Counselor and Mighty God, Everlasting father, Prince of Peace, and the Wonderful Counselor, Mighty God. Your reign shall never end." You can now begin to see the great mystery of creation through the lens of objective hope. You can rest your eyes on my words. You will find fulfillment when you put them into practice. All things are within you!

68.   Although you are taught that everything is created by your consciousness, what you accept and believe will be externalized and molded in your environment. You will witness the state that you accept in all the circumstances you encounter.

69.   Because you have unlimited imagination, all things are possible. Imagine you are what you want. Imagine yourself being the person you desire to be. You have taken on a virtue that you didn't have by subjectively appropriating your objective hope. Ask no one for help.

70.   The feeling of certainty that it instills can help you determine the truth of any idea. It doesn't matter how others think. If you can see the world exactly as you want it to be, you will find inspiration to believe it. It doesn't matter what it is, if you are clear about what you want, then you can make that desire real and natural. You will feel a sense of certainty that no power can stop. Once you feel that way, don't hesitate to let go. Do not ask others if you did the right thing. You did it, and that is all that matters.

71.   "Fear not, although you meant evil against my family, but God intended it for good." When there's time to think about the act, everything works out for the good of all. I could return to my small family. It seemed like the end of the world came at a certain point in our lives. My father's business partners wanted to control the equity that he had and so they succeeded. Our world fell apart. Our friends and family had little, so we were left with nothing. What appeared to be an evil thing ended up being a blessing. We were able to separate ourselves from the partnership.. They

were small because they couldn't think large. . My father was the first to start on his own, with sons who could think.Our family has made our business a multi-faceted enterprise with many types of businesses, without any outside partners. This is far more than we could have imagined possible 40 years ago. We can now see the benefits. It took time and reflection. . Although my father's friends intended to do evil against me, . God intended it to be good.

72.   The redeeming power of man is imagination. This is the power referred to in the Bible as "the Second Man". "The Lord from Heaven" This power is also embodied in Christ Jesus, the man who gave it to us.

73.   Tell me what you want. I won't tell you the way to get it. Tell me what you want and I might hear you say that you have it. I will not listen to you if you tell me what your dream is. Man is adamant about talking about his problems. Man enjoys reciting his problems and can't believe that all he has to do is to state his desires clearly. You will stop dwelling on your problems if you believe imagination creates reality.

74.   Every dream contains within itself the capacity for symbolicsignificance. The symbol for the power of imagination is the fish. Your imagination will take you to the depths of despair. Your imagination will help you get out of the hole. Your imagination will not be fed if you get lost in the reasoning world. Reason negates your flow. Christ, your human imagination is not bound by the reasoning world. All things are possible for him. You feed Christ if you ignore the facts and live in your imagination as if your wishes were already fulfilled.

75.	All efforts are made to awaken the imagination.

76.	You have to believe that imagination can create reality. I challenge you to think of a state which would allow you to fulfill your desires. It doesn't matter what others think, it's your thoughts that count. What does it matter if someone else thinks differently than you?

77.	The Bible is more than beautiful poetry. It is God's inspired word. Is it not possible to imagine yourself somewhere else when you lay down on your back and pretend you're there? Imagine yourself as God and you will be able to escape the dark caverns within your body by imagining. . All imagination . You can't die.It is impossible to go to eternal death with something that cannot die. Your immortality is imagination. You are the core of scripture. . Jesus Christ, the Lord God Jehovah. . Who came here to fulfill a purpose. You must pay the price for living in Caesar's world. While you may be critical of our politicians or protest any increase in taxes, you will still be taxed. You only need to learn how to pray and make more money. A story about the late President Kennedy is what brings back memories. His father was. . who, in a single generation, had made more than four-hundred millions dollars. . He complained that his children were overspending. Kennedy stated at a banquet that the only way to solve this problem was for fathers to earn more money.

A friend of mine told me one day that her father used to say, "If you had but a dollar, and it was necessary for your child to spend it, do it as if it were an empty leaf. Then you will be the owner of a vast forest." One who is truly able to pray can spend his dollar, then make it again. This world was created by the imagination of man, so it's important to understand the secrets of prayer. Stop wishing if you still have the desire. What would it be like if your dream became a reality? What would it feel like to be the person you want to be? When you feel that feeling, it is time to start thinking from it. The secret to prayer is to think from rather than thinking about. This will allow you to know your location, bank balance, job, credit cards, friends, and loved ones. . As you think from this state.

You can still move to another country and have the same experience of reality if you practice and discover the great secret of praying. Keep my message in your heart and follow it. If you practice the art of praying daily, you will eventually find that the most effective prayer you can say is "Thank You Father." This will allow you to feel the God-given power within yourself. It can be described as "thou", but you will also know that it is "I." Once this happens, you will have a thou/I relationship and then say, "Thanks Father!" Because all thoughts spring from Him, I can know that I have a desire for something if I ask him. He has granted me the desire, and I am grateful for it. I then walk in faith, knowing that the one who gave it me through the mediums of desire will make it bodily for me to experience in the flesh. Do not get into the habit of judging, criticizing and seeing only the unloved.

You can live a full life. . Live it well. It's so much easier to be kind, generous, loving, and kind than to judge. Let others do the same if they want. These are a part of you that you still have to overcome, but don't let them get in the way. Just thank your Heavenly Father for this amazing drama. At the end, the supreme actor will emerge from it all, and you will be able to see that He is you.

78.   I could lift a Stradivarius in the hands of someone who can play the violin, but I would soon be driven insane if I gave the same instrument to someone who cannot. The violin is the same, but one can bring harmony and the other can cause discord. The same instrument can be used to kill or make alive your imagination. There will be many discords before you learn how to play. We are learning how to play the instrument that is God in this world of educated darkness. Although you may not be able to find anyone willing to give you $10,000, if you believe that all things are possible with God, and you also know that God is your human imagination and can create the world you want, you can still imagine yourself having the money. Keep believing and you will get it. I don't know how, but I know it will be done according to your beliefs.

79.   This was the day I discovered this amazing truth. . Everything in my world is ananifestation of the mental activity that goes on inside me. The conditions and circumstances that I live in only reflect my state of consciousness. . It is the most important in my life.

80.   Are you a believer that God can do all things? Do you believe that God is your amazing human imagination? You may not believe that God is all-love and that you can imagine unlovely things. However, if God isn't all-powerful, then you don't have to be all-knowing. You can see things that God cannot. You can create discord and harmony by imagining God striking only harmonious notes. Your amazing human imagination is what makes all things possible. It can kill and make alive, and it can wound and heal. You may be able to create what you don't want by learning how to believe in your imagination. While you may inflict some injuries on your own, you can create the opposite in your imagination.

81.   Believe me, imagining does create reality. I mean it. The secret to imagining is the key to understanding Jesus. Believe in your imagination if you truly believe in God. It is the power and wisdom of God. You will find only one power in all of the universe, and that is me. It is called God or Jesus. If you see Jesus as an outsider, someone who lived 2,000 year ago, you won't ever know him. If you view God as an impersonal force, you will never know him. God is a person because of you. As he became you, so we can become like Him. You can take my message and use it to your advantage. You can become the man you want to be. Do not dream about it. Be present and aware of it. Don't worry about meeting the "right" people. These people are just reflections of what you do. You can change your thinking and the behavior of others around you.

82.	An imaginal act can be described as an objective, immediate fact. An imaginal act, which is based on low-intensities like we are, can be realized over a time period. So every vision that is there, I assume that it is me. But at the moment my senses and reason deny that it is me, I still assume that I am. If I believe it and it feels real and natural to me, I know that I have planted it. Then it will come back to life when it is broken. Each vision is unique and has its own time of gestation. The prophet tells us that every vision is different. It ripens, flowers, but if it seems slow, then it is certain, it won't be late." When you can see the image clearly in your mind's eyes, it will appear as objective as the room now. . Again, I speak from personal experience.I suddenly found myself sitting in my home chair, or on my couch or bed. . Without my eyes being open physically. . I see a world I wouldn't see if it weren't for my physical location. And I don't want to deny it. It is just as real as you. It is objective and it seems solidly real. I enter the world I see and consciousness follows my vision. It closes around me and the world that I thought was the only one I should know is closed to me. I am now part of the world that I imagined, it is mine. It is as real as the world I have just explored.

83.	You will be able to test your imagination and find out if you were the cause of the world's response.

84.	Every thing you see in your world, even if it seems outside, is inside your imagination. Christ Jesus is the center of this amazing imagination. The actual habitation of all things is in imagination. It doesn't matter what you see around the world; it all comes from your imagination.

85.	However, I do know that Gods law is applicable to Caesar's world. Although I don't know the time it takes for an egg to hatch in a nest of eggs, I know that each one will hatch at its own pace. As it is with assumptions. Although I don't know how long it will take to become wealthy, I can be certain that I will feel rich when I do. Conception is my goal. My inner conviction that it is possible depends on how long it takes for me to believe it is possible. It takes twelve months to breed a horse, nine months for a cow, and twenty-one days for a chicken. But, there are also intervals. The truth about every concept can only be known through the certainty of the feeling. It is impossible to disturb your knowledge of it if you don't know it!

86.   The unawakened imagination is not an idea, but a sleeping man's idea.

87.   You will be able to create a mental drama that implies you have achieved your goal. Then close your eyes, focus your attention inwardly, and then take part in the predetermined action.88. It is the height of wisdom to realize that there is only one destiny in the universe. This is because it is created by man's imagination. The mind of man has the only power. The imagination of man creates him.

89.   Gazing at an object fixedly may be helpful if you find it difficult to direct your attention when in a state similar to sleep. Don't look at the surface of an object, but instead, look into and beyond any objects with depth, such as walls, carpets, or other plain surfaces. It should reflect as little light as possible. Then imagine that you can see and hear what you desire until your attention is only occupied with the imagined state. When you wake up from your dream state, you will feel like you have returned from a faraway place.This visible world, which you thought was closed off, is now present and telling you that you were deceived into believing the object of your contemplation was true. But if you are committed to your vision, your visions will become tangible concrete facts in your world if you keep your mind focused on them. Identify your highest ideal, and focus your attention on it until you are able to identify with it. Feel the sensation of being it. . If you were to embody it in your life, this would be the feeling that you have. Although you may have denied it, your senses will still insist on this assumption. . It will be a reality in your life. Simply by looking at the people

around you, you will see when you have achieved the desired state of consciousness.

This is a great way to check in with yourself, as your mental conversations can reveal more about you than your physical conversations. Talking with people in your mind the same way you did before is a sign that you are not changing your self-perception. All changes in self-perceptions result in a change in how you relate to the world. Remember the old saying, "What you see when looking at something is not dependent on what's there but on what you assume when you look at it." The assumption that the wish has been fulfilled should help you to see the world as if it were a physical reality. Through the language of desires, the spiritual man speaks to the human being. You can achieve success in life and fulfillment of your dreams by listening to the voice.

It is a sign that the wish has been fulfilled by your unwavering obedience to it. To want a state, is to have it. Pascal stated, "You wouldn't have sought me if you hadn't already found me." Man can change his future by believing that the wish has been fulfilled, and then living and acting upon this conviction. Freedom loving individuals have the unalienable right to "change their future". The divine discontent within man that drives him to greater and higher levels is what would prevent the world from moving forward.

90.   Satan is the doubter. He is the one who doubts the reality and existence of your imaginalacts. You can't believe that your unseen imaginal act is real, so you might believe in another person. But you will always be imagining. . Imagine. . The power of the universe is yours. You heard it all in the beginning, but your inner ears will tell you what you are seeing, and you'll find that everything you take from the world will come back to you one hundred times.

91.   Let me tell you, before you came into this world of tribulations and death, you were God the Father. But you didn't know it. To know that the entire world and everything within it is yours, you had to experience this experience. It is all God's. The only way to know that it is yours is by becoming the Father. Although you might be able to own the earth, you would not be able to know all of it. You could even starve if you didn't know how to take it.

92.   You pictured yourself as the person you want to be, and your friends were happy for you. Christ was speaking to you from the outside, rational self. Your own amazing human imagination is telling you Christ that he knows that you are afraid and that you have obligations. But that it doesn't matter because "I will go to prepare a place"! He is the one who will prepare the state.

93.   Blake compared the human imagination to the divine body of Lord Jesus Christ. He said: "Babel mocks God by saying that there is no God or son. But thou, O human imagination and O divine body art all delusion. But I know thee O Lord." He knew exactly what he had seen and how he got back to the mundane world called the waking state. . When he opened his tired eyes,. . That he had been returned. He was able to imagine what he saw in the other realm. And he understood the power of his creator.He understood that imagination is the key to all things. Without imagination, nothing was ever made. You can control your dreams if you are able to wake up in a dream and identify the person imagining it. This is also true for the real world. It is also a dream. Awake! Control your day by remembering who is creating it. You will eventually wake up and realize that all you see is what your imagination has created. You came here to expand, and the restriction you placed on yourself was there for expansion.

94.	You have never seen anything happen that wasn't your imagination. You can do anything you desire, but you must have sincere desires to achieve your goal. It must be something you truly desire and that you are prepared to change your position. It is not possible to believe that you can have what you want for just a moment, and then go back to the old state. This is because you will be a double-minded person and you will not receive any help from the (Imagining Lord), as the Book of James teaches us. You can be successful in business if you want. It doesn't matter how many creditors or bank statements you have. If you believe success and continue to believe that you can succeed, you will never fail. This is the law that governs our lives.

95.	Do you remember the story about the prodigal child? The Father did not abandon the first son, but the father of the second was. . Asking to be given the. . He went out into the world and lost everything. After the second son had experienced the world of death, he remembered his Father and turned around. The Father gave the Father the robe and the ring, and prepared a fattened calf for a reception to honor his son, who had returned. The Father replied to the first son, "Son, I am always with you." The Father said, "Son, you have never separated yourself from me. All that is mine is yours." This was the reason the first son didn't know anything about the power of imagination. He didn't know how he could take it all.If you didn't know, you could have a million dollars in the bank tonight and still die from starvation. You have all that the Father has, but you won't know until you use your imagination and take it. Both you and I have left the Father. He chose to make us suffer in this world of futility. In the hope of releasing us from the world of decay, where everything dies and allowing us to enjoy the glorious liberty of the children of God, he did it. . Those who use their imagination with love.

96.   You must take me seriously. Take me seriously! Believe that the reality you envision is possible. It will become a fact at this level if you believe in it. When the image is complete, you will be able to return to your ancestral self and there will no need for time between the act of imagining and the reality.

97.   Perhaps a friend of mine is unwell. Or maybe he's not working or earning enough money to cover his obligations. He is still in me. He is in me, as I think about him. I don't need him to be physically present in order to think about him. He is always within me. He is in me; I think about him. Can I alter his whole picture in my mind? I think he is speaking to me and telling me that he has never experienced more and that he has never felt happier. As I believe what I see in my mind's eye, I can change his entire picture. . I believe in him. Christ is in me. All things are possible for Christ. Test it, and then see if it works. If you don't see him in the near future earning more and looking better, then he will respond to everything you have done. You don't have to praise him or thank you.His praise is not necessary; you do not need his thanks. He doesn't need to confirm anything, except that he accepts what you have done for him. You don't need to ask anyone to thank you. You don't have to say thank you. You are simply exercising the power within you of God. Jesus Christ is the power and wisdom of God. There is no other world than God. It is all God you have "pushed out", and God is your amazing human imagination. He cannot be further away. God is always near. Nearness does not mean separation. He is not separated. God literally became what I am, so that I might be like Him.

He is not like the outside. He cannot touch me, no matter how close He gets. He became me with all my flaws, all my limitations. Now I'm trying to discover who I really am, which is His name. My name is in Him. What is your name? "Go and say that I AM sent you." "Yes, forever forever it is my name." Jehovah?" "No." The Lord?" "No. I AM." That is His name. This is His name forever and ever.

98.	Imagine if the Lord (or your imagination) claimed that David is (the world) always does his will and you could, with a simple act of imagination, command the outside world to do the same. . Are you not the Lord?

99.	Keep believing in your imagination and the world will respond. The world does not cause. It only responds to your imagination. Only God can act, and only you can imagine God acting. Try it before you decide. You can't fail if you try it. And when you have demonstrated imagination during the testing, please share your good news with your brothers. You can show everyone how the world works. This principle can be applied to anyone, regardless of their social or educational background.

100.	The Christ-in-man, Imagination, does not have to produce only the perfect and best. It is free from the necessity of producing the right things.QUOTES 101- 200

101.	If you see a situation from the outside, it will become entangled in your shadows. . Everybody who responds to your imaginative act is a shadow. How is a shadow able to cause something in your world? You give someone else the power to cause, and you are transferring the power to him. Other people are just shadows who witness what is happening within you. Your actions are forever reflected in the world. Once you realize this, you will be free to create the story of your salvation.

102.   Let's make it a habit to control and discipline our imagination every day. Imagine better than what you know. No coal of character is so hard that it cannot glow and flame when slightly turned. Do not blame, but instead resolve. Like music, life can be transformed by a new setting to make all its discords harmonious. Your friend should be able to express the things he wants to. Let's face it, no matter how we approach another person, we will be approached with a similar attitude. How can we achieve this? Do the same thing as my friend. Call your friend mentally to establish rapport.Mentally call his name, focusing your attention on him. This will be like calling his name if you were to catch his attention in a public place. Mentally hear his voice when he answers. . Imagine that he is telling your story about the good things you wish for him. Tell him, in turn, how happy you are to have witnessed his good fortune. After you have mentally heard the news that you desired, and are thrilled by it, you can go about your day.

The end must be accepted by your imagined conversation. The acceptance of the end is the only way to devise effective ways. Even the most wisest reflection could not come up with better solutions. Your conversation with your friend should not be distorted by doubts about the truth of the things you believe you are hearing and saying. You will soon discover that your imagination is allowing you to hear and say all you have ever heard or said. Habits are what we are made of; they act like the most powerful law in the universe.

You can transform your world with this knowledge of the power and potential of imagination. Be a disciplined man by being able to imagine and feel only the good. You will be able to inspire others with the beautiful idea that you have awakened in yourself. Don't wait for four months to reap the rewards. Today is the best day to learn how to control your imagination. The only thing that limits man is his ability to pay attention and limit his imagination. Controlled imagination and sustained attention that is focused firmly on the goal are the keys to success.

103.   He knows that every desire is ripe grain for him who can think from the end. Therefore, he is not influenced by mere reasonable probability. He is confident that his imagination will make his assumptions solid.

104.   Because they don't know how to concentrate and condense their power to penetrate the thin crust, men believe in the external world. It is quite easy to see this view of the senses, strangely. We don't have to exert much effort to remove the veil from the senses; the objective world disappears when we focus our attention on it. It is enough to focus on the state we want to mentally see. But, to make it a reality so it becomes an objective fact, it is necessary to keep our eyes fixed upon that state until it has all of the sensory vividness and sensations of reality.Concentrated attention makes our desire seem to have the distinctness and feel of reality. When the form of our thought is as vivid and real as nature, it has the right to be a tangible fact in our lives. Every man must choose the best way to focus his attention on the desired state and control it. Meditation is my preferred state. It's a more relaxed state than sleep but still allows me to control my imagination and fix my attention on something.

105.   Only the imaginative image is worth searching for.

106.   Nothing can stand between you and that foundation, which Paul speaks of and describes as the creative power and wisdom of God. You can't let anyone stand between you and God. God is your amazing human imagination and who can guide you there? You think every moment of your day. You will get rewarded if your thoughts survive fire. Your imagination (your thought) is fireproof. If fulfillment is dependent on another person or chain letters, going to church, and praying to an unidentified God, then you have something in your way. You and the Lord Jesus Christ must not be separated by your imagination (thought).

107.   Although it may be surprising to you to identify the central figure in the Gospels with human imagination, I am certain you will soon realize that this is what the ancients meant. However, man has misread the Gospels and his biography as history and cosmology and has fallen asleep to the power within him.

108.	Through the sense of feeling, imagine your desire. That assumption,subjectively appropriated and believed to be true, is faith. Is it possible to believe that this is true? Can you convince yourself that all things are possible for him who believes? Blake said in his amazing "Marriage of Heaven and Hell": "I dined at Isaiah and Ezekiel and inquired: Does a strong conviction that a thing exists, make it so?" Isaiah responded: It does. All prophets believe so. In ages of imagination, a firm persuasion could move mountains. But many people today are incapable of a firm persuasion. Everything was once a wish, then believed. The building, clothes, and car you drive are all first desires that were then realized.109. The man of imagination realizes that the world is a manifestation his mental activity, so he tries to control and determine the ends of his thoughts.

110. Forgiveness is actually experiencing in your imagination the revised version, what you wish that you had in the flesh.

111.	To light your path in the world, you have to go outside. Although you may light a candle, a lamp or use electricity, one day you'll discover that you are the true light of the universe. You will then realize that you are God, the light with infinite love, infinite power and infinite wisdom. As you overcome the barriers of reason, senses, and will begin to expand into these states. You are challenged to think about yourself. Is your mind firmly set on the ideal state? You can test yourself and, in doing so, you will be testing Christ (imagination), who is God's wisdom and power. You don't have to pay anything to test him. So, give it a shot.

112.	Your desires can help you test your creativity. It is possible to desire something that you can't afford or don't know how to enjoy. There are many reasons why it is impossible to possess. . It is true that imagination can create reality. . You can visualize it. It is enough to imagine it. You must believe that the reality will come true. You must believe that you are the person you envision. Then wait for it to happen in your world. It will grow and blossom. It will ripen and flower if it seems too long. . It is not too late to wait.

113.   A change in consciousness is what the mystic refers to as "death", not the destruction or fusion of imagination and state, but the dissolution thereof.

114.   You can either believe in your amazing human imagination or you don't, because that is Christ. Although an event occurred 2,000 years ago it is unlikely that it will ever happen again. Every believer and hearer of his birth can see it in their lives. What are you to do? Believe in the one he sent. I didn't come to the world to convince you that I was a holy man. I came to the world to let you know that I had woken from my dream of living. II have completed the race. I've fought the good fight and kept my faith. It doesn't matter if I take off this shirt, because this world is over. In the hope of convincing you, I'll tell you about my experiences while I'm here. . Neville is not the right place, but your amazing human imagination who you sent. Your true name is I AM and your creative power can be called Jesus Christ. Your imagination is the key to all things. Take a look at yourself and find out. Your imagination is your greatest asset.

115.   Tonight will be both a practical and spiritual hour for you, as I speak to the Creator. Paul wrote to the Romans: "All the inexplicable things of God can be clearly seen, being comprehended by the things which are made." To see the made, man is required to search for the invisible God. How? By questioning himself. Take a look around and ask yourself if there were times when you believed in the future but didn't have any support. You have discovered the Creator to be your amazing human imagination if you can recall. Could this be God? Paul then claims that they didn't honor God even though they knew God.Do you consider your imagination to be God after discovering the connection between the things seen, and the imaginal act? Do you look at images that resemble mortal man, birds or animals and think they are the cause? You are denying the truth of God and worshipping the creator if you believe that something outside is responsible for your good fortune or your misfortune. Instead, try to relate your outer world with an inner imaginal activity. If you don't accept that God is the cause for everything in your outer world then you are not honoring your imagination as God.

116.   Also, man cannot "die" when he wears the garment he has worn. However, the Being that He really is is only imagination. As He enters, whatever He enters takes on cubic reality. This I have proved. The Immortal You can't die. It didn't begin. It didn't begin. . You are somewhere else from the moment you leave. But, because you're there, it becomes cubic reality. It is as real as the world around it. It is terrestrial just like this world. And no one can "die" in this world. Everything lives in your amazing human imagination. Now, the purpose of life is to awaken this Being within you so that He is fully aware at all times. This is the purpose and meaning of life. He who came down to accept the limitations and weaknesses of the garment and kept them there, is bound to wake up while He walks on this earth. This earth is what I mean to my senses. But it doesn't end at the point where my senses stop registering it. It doesn't end at "death," as the Being within it continues to exist and is still part of the world. However, His entry into it gives it a cubic reality like this room because He is in it.

117.   You are the God of scripture, who is your amazing human imagination. Your own amazing human imagination is the only god.

118.   It is possible to be everything you want, because the believerand God of the universe are one. You can't separate yourself from God. He is your I AMness. You can never achieve your dreams if you don't believe in your I AMness. You can only achieve your goals if you believe you are already the person you want to be. It's that simple.

119.   Although I can't give you all the atoms in my body, it is mine. I couldn't tell if you took my hand off that it was mine, but I can tell you what you look at. Yet, I know you are "pushed out" because this body is the body that I wear. So, my body will obey me, and you will follow my mind. It is up to me to focus on what I want from this world and to follow the Golden Rule: Doing unto others only the things I would like done to me; not hurting anyone, and doing no other thing than the things I would like done to me. Do only the beautiful things if you want to see all the wonderful things happen. Then, use your amazing human imagination to do all the rest. This is how you can discover the incredible secret of imaging. It is the greatest secret of all secrets and the one to which everyone should strive, since Christ is the answer.

120.   Recently, a friend shared with me a vision in which I appeared. He said: "The story about Jesus is persistent assumption." If true, then we are instructed to imitate Jesus as a child. I must be bold enough to believe that I am what I want to become. I will continue to believe that until I am objectively able to realize the truth of what I've assumed. If I am one with all, then how can anyone be more than me? Don't believe someone is more than you simply because they have an influx of spirit and validity. Your imagination is the only God and there is no higher being than Him. You are the one you desire to be. Keep believing that. Keep playing that role until you see the results of your actions.

121.   Believe in the reality that you create. Faith is loyalty to an unseen reality. Believe in the reality of your imaginal acts. Your loyalty to the unseen world will allow the outside world to see what is not there.

122.   All that I'm saying to you comes from the Bible. "I kill and makealive. I can heal and I wound, and there is no one that can take my hand. I, I AM He and there is no God apart from me. I AM the Lord, your God, the holy one in Israel, your Savior, and there is no other savior. These are   God's words, as revealed by his prophets. The New Testament fulfills their prophecy as follows: "Whatever you want, believe that you have received it." This is how easy it is to apply it. A false assumption can be denied by your senses but if you persist in believing it will become a fact.

123.   Your I AMness, He. Speak: "I AM secure, wealthy, and free." Although this may not be true according to your senses, I am asking you to simply say the words. For the moment that you do, you are subjectively appropriating wealth, security, and freedom. These will be taken from you by Reason, so I invite you to play a game with me. Walk through the door as if you were secure, rich, and free. As if it were true, you will sleep this night. You will not go to sleep seeing the world the same way you saw it last night. You would feel $20,000 more rich if someone handed you a check for $20,000 this morning and you put it in your account. Don't wait for someone to give you the money. Get into bed and start living as if it were true. You can put Christ to the test. Can you believe that all things can be done by God? I don't guarantee you will succeed overnight, or even in the next day. You may have difficulty believing what you can believe because you were trained to accept only the truth of your senses and reason. . but you can!

124.   Before anything can be made a reality, it must first be imagined. God is that ability to imagine.

125.   Even if you make terrible mistakes, everything can be solved. Do not be ashamed of what you have done, will do or might do. As you learn to play the instrument that is God and your amazing human imagination, there is no other creative power.

126.   It is possible to be the man or woman you desire, but it takes more than wishing. It takes effort to see the world as it is and make it yours. When it does, you should continue to do so until you feel the truth of what you see, touch, taste, smell, and hear. . And then, explode! You will be pregnant! What do you do with your pregnancy? Nothing! It will just appear when it is most convenient for you. It will. It will happen when you least expect it. Your desire will manifest in the world around you, whether you are looking for fame, wealth, health, or fame. This is how God's law works.

127.   If someone is born in poverty and dreams of great wealth, it seems natural that he will achieve his dream. You are dreaming. You are likely to have a nervous breakdown if you try to make your dreams come true but doubt its possibility. If you believe in your amazing claim, it is possible to fulfill it. You are the God of which the Bible speaks.

128.   Only one reality exists, and that is Christ. . Human Imagination is the inheritance and ultimate achievement of all of Humanity.

129.   You are saying that you can afford $400 per month rent now if you say "I remember when it was difficult to afford it." You have overcome that limitation by saying, "I remember when it was difficult to live on my monthly income." By remembering when, you can get yourself in any condition. It is possible to recall when your friend expressed her desire for marriage. You can recall when your friend was single and convince yourself that she is not in that situation anymore.

130. Man thinks that everything outside of him is the cause in his infant years.The phenomena of life. Astrology is a popular belief. I have to admit that I once believed in astrology. An old friend of mine was a retired teacher who taught me astrology. She became an astrologer to increase her retirement income. One day, I found her in tears. She was probably sitting near an open window, and a breeze blowing through the papers caused her to draw the chart for a man ten years older than her customer. She didn't realize it, but she believed that. . The man is. . His business venture would succeed.

If this was true, the customer promised to send her $100. Norma was able to see in the chart the message the man wanted, and she believed her little hieroglyphics. It was all that matters. The rest was easy for her to do. The foundation of this is: "Whatever your heart desires, believe that you can get it." This was the time that I had grown out of my belief in monkey bones and teacup leaves, astrology, numerology or any other form of human imagination. I tested my beliefs and found that everything was possible. I couldn't console Norma, even though I had told her. The man promised $100, but I was there to help her receive a check from Western Union. Norma knew the truth about the one foundation. Astrology brought her a small amount of income so she remained a professional astrologer up to her death. Norma isn't the only one. Many ministers, priests, and teachers know that the teachings he gives are false, but they refuse to believe in the one foundation: human imagination.

131.   If man can see Christ in his imagination, he will understand why Christ must die and rise from the dead to save him. . He must remove his current state from his imagination and use it to create a higher version of himself in order to rise above his limitations and save himself.

132.   I now ask you to keep testing your creativity. . imagination. . Revision is something you can do. Do not accept something you don't love. Instead, revise it immediately. Listen to the words that should have been said and convince yourself that it is true.

133.   It is time for man not to believe in the external world and instead, to believe in his own imagination. It is time to end all external icons. "You will not make any graven image of me or have any other gods than me, but your wonderful human imagination. It doesn't matter if you don't have a lot of education or money, or if it is difficult to believe in yourself. But because everything is possible for him who believes, and God is all-powerful, you can believe anything to be possible. You can test your imagination and see if it performs?

134.   Do not ask yourself if your qualifications are valid. Instead, consider whether you really want the item. Don't worry about when or how it will happen. Just assume that it is already happening and that it will be done in a way no one else knows. You will see your business grow, and your family grow. Everything will turn out exactly as you imagined. You can move so fast that you can't stand still, and you can see exactly where you want to be. It has happened to me. My sister in Barbados wanted to see me, even though I was physically 2,000 km away. I used my imagination and moved in my mind. She saw me lying on her bed when she entered her room.She wrote me the day before and shared her story. I now know that all things can be achieved,

because God and you are one. I stand by my words. Motion is the only way to bring about anything. The motion is already within you. You know exactly what you want. So, look at the world with the assumption that you already have it. If the world is the same, you have not moved. Only when the change can be seen can you tell that you have moved. Keep thinking about the new state. Motion can only be detected by a change in position relative to another object. Referring to a friend can be a great reference point. Let him look at you the way he would if your wish were realized. He wouldn't see you any other way, would he? Accept his congratulations if he would. Mentally extend your hand and feel the reality in his hand. Listen to his words of congratulations and feel the reality. Have faith in your unseen reality. It will not stop you from living your life.

135.   Recognizing the power and importance of feeling, let's pay close attention to our moods and attitudes. The exercise of imagination and feeling is key to man's progression at every stage. We can create an "ideal" in our mental sphere and feel ourselves becoming one with it. By the intensity of his imagination or feeling, the solitary or captive can affect myriads. He can speak through many people and act through many women. Trust your senses, extend your reach, feel your feelings, and don't be afraid to express your emotions. To feel the good of another person, you must be more aware. You can be like my friend and feel more for the health, wealth, happiness, and well-being you want. If ideas don't descend from Heaven, they aren't blessed. Results or achievements are the key test of imagination. These results will help you to decide to fill your images of love and to live in a noble and high-spirited mood.

136.   Some people try to hurry everything into existence. Some people try to force birth from conception. But it is impossible. Many experiences are not documented in scripture. I'm not here to judge anyone on whether or not they have. However, I know from personal experience that if you believe you can be what you want, your inner conviction and your feeling of certainty will make it happen. You have accepted the desired state and it will come to pass. It will mature and blossom. It will ripen and flower even if the state is slow to objectify itself.

137.   You, the Word, sent yourself into the world as the fulfillment of all you promised. You were the Word that was with God in the beginning. You are God's Word. Your words will never be void. You brought the pattern of salvation with you when you emerged from the knowledge that you are the Father. This pattern you will follow, for it is the one that brings you back to the Father knowledge you've been searching. By falling asleep to your true awareness, you were able to escape from yourself and enter the world of men. When you trust God, your amazing human imagination, and the only God, you will be able to return to that awareness. You don't need to be distracted by the small things. God is all you need. If you say "I AM", you speak as God. You can limit an infinite being by adding any word. The infinite, which is limitless, follows his own law and becomes the unlimited being he believes he is. . Whether it is unwanted, sick, helpless or poor. Be confident in the world you create and believe in yourself. . Because all things can be imagined. . Once you are aware of something, it has the power to project onto your screen.

138.   You are helping God by representing another person to yourself. When your time is up, you'll enter the temple to find the sign of your creative power being born as a baby wrapped in swaddling clothing. The arm of God, the creator of all things, will then be revealed in you. From that day forward, whatever you can imagine will come true. . It doesn't matter what it is. This thought is my request. Please ponder it and follow the example of Simon. You can lift the burden of another person today and tomorrow. Do not let someone else carry your burden. There is no one else. Take the burden off of him and follow Jesus Christ, your amazing human imagination.

139.   Prayer is the raising of the mind towards the goal. Always "arise" is the first word that should be corrected. Lift your mind towards the goal. You can do this by believing that your wish has been fulfilled. What would it feel like to have your prayer answered? Imagine that you could feel the same feeling if your prayers were answered. Prayer is about taking action mentally. Prayer is about focusing your attention on the fulfillment of a wish until it overwhelms your mind and takes all other thoughts out of your consciousness. Although prayer can be described as a mental activity that involves focusing on the desire fulfilled until it fills your mind and crowds out all other thoughts, this does not mean prayer is only a mental effort. . An act

of will. Prayer is, on the contrary. Prayer is surrender. It is a surrender to the desire of fulfilling a wish. If prayer brings no response . . There is something wrong in the prayer, and it is usually due to too much effort. It is dangerous to confuse the state of prayer with an action of will. If you observe this rule, you will naturally fall in line with the sovereign rule.

140.   Move out of the state that is prone to poverty and into one that is rich. Wealth will become a reality. Because you think from it, this room has substance and reality. However, a room is only a shadow. A state is a possibility that seems impossible. It is only possible to enter the state by thinking from it. Blake stated that if the spectator could only enter the image in his imagination, and if he could make friends and companions of his image, he'd rise from the grave to meet the Lord in heavens. You are now a spectator of others states if you are buried in one state. If you can rise from your current state and burrow yourself in another, it will be a way to express your desires. You can become what you desire. You don't have to stay in the same place you are unhappy in and continue to argue when you can imagine a different state. Once you've achieved the state of your fulfillment, don't look back like Lot's wife. Salt is a preservative, so don't look back at the state you were in.

141.   This simple technique can bring everything into existence. In my desire to visit my family in Barbados I slept in New York City like I was in Barbados. I thought of New York City 2,000 miles north. My brother wrote a letter approving the trip, and enclosed a draft to pay for my expenses. Although I hadn't written to my brother asking for the money, I was still physically asleep in New York City, and I was imagining myself in Barbados when my brother felt the urge to write to me and tell me why I should return home. The family required me to complete the link as I hadn't been back in 12 years. I was able to justify his letter, justification for the draft, and the expense he would incur. . Without a nickel . Simply imagined that I was already in Barbados. I knew exactly what I had done and I believe all things are made by God. . Imagination . Without him, there is no thing made that is made. So I have come to believe God is my human imagination. Do I want to fall for the trap of not honoring him (Imagination), but instead turn to an image that resembles a human being to claim he caused my trip? Do I want to credit my brother for sending me the draft? And notifying the steamship company that I wanted a ticket, or do you think it is better to just give credit

to him? Or will I remember the God? . Imagination . That I found? Paul asks everyone who reads his letter this question. Are you going to honour God as God after finding God? Or will you trade the truth about God in exchange for a lie?

142.   The Bible starts with this line: "In the beginning God created heavens and earth." This is where we can see that God created the inside (for God says that heaven is within and God is at his heaven) as well as the outside. He also created the earth which is not. If the earth is outside, and God is inside, how did God create it? The act of movement: "The spirit and power of God moved upon all the waters." This shows that motion is the cause and that it is impossible for anything to be produced without it. How does God move? The act of imagining.Motion can only be detected if there is a change in a reference frame. What would it take to get from where you are to where you want to go? What would your friends think of you if there was a change? What would your outside world look like? Spend some time imagining what you want. How can you tell if you've moved? Mentally looking at the world around you and noticing its changes.

143.   The Book of Psalms tells you to "Comune with yourself." Sit quietly. Relax and be at peace with your thoughts. Then, you will find that God's thoughts suddenly flow through you. You were God in the beginning! In the end, God will reunite you and me with the entire world of billions. One imagination was lost in this world of appearing others, but the whole is within us all. The enemies of a man are his family, as they all exist within him. Man fights within him until he recognizes that there is only one, and that there is nothing else. In the hope of convincing himself, he then tells others. As he rises from within he is called back to the one Being he was before the world existed. God intended for God to expand into unity by causing division.

144.   Get started now and put your imagination to work. Jesus Christ is within you, and you won't fail if God calls your desires forth with His name. Assume that you are already the person you want to be and expect evidence to show up in your life. "I AM THE TRUE VINE" is the last bold statement of the Book of John. If God's name, I AM, is synonymous with God Himself then I am. . The vine . Will grow and produce the fruits I am aware of. You must be aware of every state you are in. You can claim the experience you want. Put your faith fully on the grace that will come to you at Christ's unveiling.Count the days until the first act occurs. Then, you'll find that the last act will be exactly 1,260 days later. You will continue to tell your story to anyone who listens. They are only interested in the things of this world, so not everyone will. Let them know how to get their stuff until they are hungry for the promise. Christ will then reveal himself to them, and they will realize that they are God the father. Yes, I AM truth, life, and the way. When I reach the end, I am the Father.

145.   You must change your imaginal activity if you want to see someone change. It is the only reason for your life. You can't believe in anything if your senses don't accept it. For nothing is impossible to imagine and imagining. . persevered in and believed. . It will make its own reality.

146.   To everyone, I say: The entire universe is in your humanimagination. You can create any wish by believing it to be true. First, know what you want. Then create the image that will fulfill it. What if your friends knew and discussed it with you? Now imagine them being with you, talking about your fulfilled dream. It could be at a dinner or cocktail party in your honor. Maybe it's just a small get-together over tea. You can create a scene in your imagination and make it real. This invisible state will create the objective state that you want, as all objective reality can only be created by imagination.

147.   Your life is nothing but the expression of your imagination. It's what you make of it.

148.   Remember that the Bible is for the man of imagination and not for mortal men.

149.   Keep revising and don't be afraid to take on the enormous responsibility of your imagination. Life is nothing but an activity of imagination. Christ is your life. I don't mean he is your imagination. Life is an activity of imagination. Find out what Christ has created by asking yourself what you're imagining now. Because imagination is the key to all things, and imagination alone is not enough to create anything.

150.   My imagination was the only God that ever existed, but I didn't feed it. Instead, I kept using the rational approach to my life and planned my life according to a reasonable plan. It was not enough to know of a power without reason; I had the responsibility to use this power within myself. Then I decided to use my imagination for myself and others. Your imagination must be used every day, morning, noon, night, and at all times. You must practice it daily to discover Christ in you, who is God The Father.

151.   Jesus' story is a fascinating mystery that can only be solved if you experience it.

152.   It is a creative act that you can experience through imagination. It is a fact in the fourth dimensions of space. It will appear in this third dimension just as easily as a seed planting will result in the growth a specific plant. It is important to not worry about the outcome of this seed you have planted in your imagination. Each seed has its own time. Some seeds take several days, others take longer. You can be confident that the seeds you have planted will eventually appear in your life. Your imagination will bring your dreams to life.

153.   Prayer is the subjective appropriation and realization of an objective hope. You can imagine giving your hope an objective reality. Bring your hope to life so that you can feel the reality of it. That feeling will fill you. . You have embraced its reality and are now ready to live it. Although the world may not instantly reflect your feelings, you can make it your reality. By making a subjective state objectively real, you have granted it your blessing. It must now fulfill its destiny in order to bless you with all you do. You can't bless your subjective hope if you don't make it a reality.Your wish will be fulfilled, so you must feel confident in your ability to clothe yourself. You are waiting for the external reality to clothe you in your desire. You will feel the feeling and be able to clothe your desire with external reality. You can now deceive your self into believing your desire is externally true, and you can give it your blessing by subjectively taking over your objective hope. It   is impossible to see what you want in your outside world. You are blind to the possibility of it. You can only eat the satisfaction that comes from living in this feeling. This feeling can be enjoyed every day, whether you are awake or asleep.

154.   Tonight take a mere wish and see it in your mind's eye as fulfilled.Contemplate it. You can merge and become completely lost in it. Your desire to become objective, to all the different tones of reality, will be granted. Break it, then return to this section to merge again. Reflect on what was real just a moment ago. You can do this and nothing on earth nor in the universe will stop you from imagining objectification. You can rest assured that it will be objectified and you can keep the Sabbath. The Sabbath is that time when you don't make any effort to make it happen, because it is already there!Don't try to take away or add to it. It will happen as soon as you decide it is good and very good. It's possible to do it. You can imagine that all things were created by God. . Then you will realize that what is completed grows out of what is accomplished. It was a wish at first, but it became a reality in the end. What is completed is what grows. The imagination is the source of all creativity in the universe. . The real man . For man is all imagination and God is God. He exists in us and in Him. The imagination is God's eternal body. The God of imagination is not distant, but a brother and friend.

155.   Now is the time to really imagine yourself as the man or woman you desire to be. Do not be afraid to doubt. Doubt is the devil. You won't become mad if you believe, regardless of what the rest of the world says, that you are the man you desire to be. You will be that man instead. Without any effort or assistance from you, your dream world will adapt to your new image.

156.   Man expresses his self through his imagination, and God expresses his self through his divine imagination. There is no clear separation between God's Imagination and man's imagination. You will be amazed to know that Imagination is God Himself. He is the divine body Jesus of which we are members. Blake claims that Divine Imagination was merged with Jesus and that Imagination made Man so that Man could become God's wisdom and power, which Blake calls Christ. False Christs other than those who are crucified, buried and rise in an individual are false. There is no Christ apart from man's amazing human imagination.

157.   According to dictionaries, meditation is defined as: fixing one's mind upon; planning in the mind; looking ahead; and engaging in continuous contemplative thought. Meditation has received a lot of misinformation. The majority of books on meditation are useless because they don't explain how it works. Meditation is simply a controlled imagination and sustained attention. Just focus on one idea and keep it there until all the other thoughts are gone. The sure sign of an inner force is the power of attention. Without distraction, we must focus on the idea that is being realized and not allow any distractions. This is the key to action. If your attention wanders, you can bring it back to the idea that you want to realize. Do this repeatedly until your attention is fixed on the idea. The idea must keep the attention. . It must be enthralling. . So to speak. The thinker is the end of meditation. He discovers that he is all he has imagined. Untrained man's attention becomes the slave of his vision, rather than the master. It is attracted by the pressing, rather than the important.

158.   Inner talking mirrors the imagination. And our imagination mirrors the state in which it is fused.

159.   Fiction is impossible. Fiction is not real today. It will become a fact tomorrow. The fiction of a book is fiction today, but it will be fact tomorrow. You can find the facts of today if you have good memory and a good research method. Every thought, however, is not recorded.

160.   My friend noticed tiny magnetic seeds that were swirling around his feet. This made the outer world seem so big. These tiny seeds of contemplative thought can be ignored or even scraped away. But awareness causes them instantly to reform and magnify the new form in the outside world. The outer world would disappear if the seeds of imagination didn't reform. But they do. Because the seeds are in man. Your thought-seeds can be rearranged to create a new pattern in your outside world. Changes in attitude are what you need to do this. You can see the world as new. By doing this, you will have removed the tiny magnetic seeds that cause their rearrangement. This is the world we live in.When imagination lifts us from the pit and places them upon the Rock, our feet are on their own. We will no longer be able to stand on the feet of others, giving them praise or blaming us. However, we can be kind, gracious, and thankful to another person for his part in our drama. We realized, however, that nothing is impossible if we are able to stand up for ourselves. . It doesn't matter if it is good, bad, or indifferent. . It is due to our attitude towards living.

161.   If your imagination is matched with your inner speech, you can find a straight line in yourself. The without will immediately reflect your inner voice, and you'll know that reality is only inner speaking.

162.   Tonight, I want you to choose the most amazing thing in the world. Find an inner conviction that it is yours. The truth of any concept can only be known through the certainty that conviction inspires. Don't be afraid to affirm that you feel confident once you do. It doesn't matter what you think. Don't be discouraged if you haven't had the same experience as me. Be confident in yourself and believe in your intuition. You can test it and see if it works.

163.   Are you clear on what you want? Here's a quick way to achieve it.Just feel the joy and continue to experience it. Keep believing in the joy of fulfillment. Tell your friends the good news in your imagination. Listen to their congratulations and then let him hear your good news. He can bring your joy of fulfillment into the world. For he who is capable of all this is within you, as your wonderful I AMness, your imagination, your consciousness. This is God. You can test God. He will not fail. Tell a friend when he performs well and keep telling them as you continue to follow this law. You can then walk knowing that all other I AM statements are yours.

This is what you can prove in the worlds of shadows. Then, in the realm of reality, the opposite will be true. Your eternal truth is your I AMness. You can declare eternal truth even though you live in a world filled with shadows. It is eternal truth to say "I AM the resurrection." "I AM life" is an eternal truth as well as "I am the way." These bold certainty preceded by the "I AM", are eternal truths. Do not listen to any person who shouts at you from the tower of Babel, telling you that there is another way. There is only one way. To get to the Cause of All Life, you don't need to give up meat or eat only fish Fridays. For there is no other God, believe in your I AMness.

164.   All things exist in the human imagination. I don't mean infinitestates. Everything you can experience now is in you, as an operant state. Only you can make a situation live. To make a state come alive, you must first enter it and then animate it. The objective reality may seem more real to you than the subjective one you entered. But, I assure you that all states exist in your imagination. A state that is subjectively entered becomes objective in your vegetative realm, where it will fade and become new again. However, its eternal form can still be revived through contemplative thought.

165.   Although you may not know who, where, and what you are, you do know who you are. You may believe you are restricted, unwanted, ignored, or mistreated, based on what your senses and reasoning tell you. Your world supports this belief. If you don't know that you are causing the mistreatment, then you will blame everyone except yourself. Yet, I can tell you that the only reason for the phenomena of life is your imaginal activity. There is no other cause.

166.   Every person, every place, and everything is animated and rearranged within; as He is so are we. That statement would be considered blasphemy by a good Christian. However, I am quoting the first epistle of the Book of John, which is the fourth chapter: "As He is, so are you in this world." This idea follows the same lines as the definition of God is love. Because God is love, He won't change your imaginal act but will allow it externalization. If God could change the act, then there would be two you: one who imagines and one who alters the imaginal act. God, who is all love, instantly plays the roles in your imaginal acts. He also suffers with you as He is dreaming. One day, Love will awaken in your skull. You will find your true identity when   he

resurrects. All of the imagery from scripture will surround your as you emerge from your immortal skull. They will see the child and witnesses, but they won't be able to see you because you will be spirit. They will witness your spiritual birth and will talk about you, but they will not see you. The great drama unfolds externally, but it is inside, because you are eternal within yourself.

167.   Man discovers his world is his mental activity madevisible. He draws others, but he cannot come to him. His first instinct is to remake the world to his ideal.

168. What makes the Bible so interesting and instructive? It is not because it addresses the Imagination, which can be described as Spiritual Sensation, but only then to the Understanding or Reason. My premise tonight will not follow any orthodox conception of Christ. Scripture is a mystery. It is God's secret that cannot be understood but must be experienced. You may be able to think that Jesus Christ, the faithful witness and the first to be born from the dead, is what you are reading in the Book of Revelation. . As the world does. . A unique being that came into this world two thousand years ago.The word "Christ" is a reference to "the Lord's Anointed." It is not one man who is called "the Lord" or another named "the anointed," but rather one person who recognizes himself as the Lord's Anointed. Who is the anointed one? Your amazing human imagination! This is the only Jesus, the only God. Blake answered a friend's question about Jesus. He said that Jesus was the only God, but that he is also me and you. Although this statement is true, man cannot accept that his human imagination is God. Blake intended his statement to be taken literally. Jesus, the Only God, is your amazing human imagination. . So am I.

169.   Simply act as God and let it happen. God said, "Let there is light. Let the sun shine." Let the moon shine! God made the moon appear after his imagination. He also supported it with faith, knowing it was impossible without faith. Faith is the assurance of what we hope for and the evidence of what we have not yet seen. You must have faith that your imagination will be realized if you believe it.

170.   Man cannot see anything other than his own consciousness. Nothing exists for us except the consciousness we have. If we do not offer our human parentsage to him, the ideal man will never be able to give birth. We are the catalyst for nature's redemption from the cruelty law. This redemption is the great purpose of consciousness. We can't accept the responsibility and point to natural laws as proving that the redemption of the world through imaginative love cannot be achieved, so we are denying the purpose of our existence. We reject the only way to accomplish this process of redemption. Only trueborn religion is worth testing. . Whether it comes from deep conviction or inner experience.A man cannot be a true believer in a religion unless it gives him an abiding feeling that everything is fine, regardless of his personal circumstances. Mental and spiritual knowledge can be achieved in completely different ways. We can see a thing from the outside and compare it with other things, analyzing it and then defining it. Whitehead defined religion as the act of a man in solitude. It is, in my opinion, what a man does with his solitude. We are driven to subjective experiences when we are alone. This is why we need to imagine ourselves as the man we want to see in the world. In solitude, we can experience what we would have experienced in real life if we had achieved our goal. We will eventually become the image of our ideal. "Renew your spirit. . Put on the new man. . "Speak every man truth with his neighbour."

It is through the "renewing our minds" that we can make a "Fact of consciousness". It is important to change your thinking. We can't change the way we think unless we have new ideas. Our thoughts are the natural output of our ideas. And our innermost thoughts are man himself. The ultimate goal of all longing is to find it. . Don't do it. Stillness is the best thing. Always strive to be. If your heart isn't in order, external reforms won't work. Heaven cannot be achieved by suppressing our passions, but by cultivating our virtues. It is not easy to forget an old idea, but it is often crowded out with new ideas. It is lost when an entirely new and compelling idea occupies our attention. It is time to let go of old ways of thinking and feeling. . Like dead oak leaves . Keep going until they are replaced by new ones.

Creativity is a higher level of receptiveness and susceptibility. Anyone who wants to change his life must make the future dream a reality. Each great out-picturing begins with a period of deep absorption. If that period of profound absorption is filled by our highest ideal, then. . When we achieve that ideal,. . Then we can see it in action and realize that the future does not disappear into the past but moves into the future. This is how we can change our future. We don't know what "now" means if it is "elsewhere". Only when "now" is also "here" can we recognize it. We can change our future when we are able to feel ourselves in the desired state of "here" as well as "now".

171.   First, many of us don't even see our harvest when it confronts us. Even if we can recall that we imagined it once, reason will tell you it would have happened anyway. Reason will remind us that we met a man at a cocktail party, who seemed to be interested in making money. He heard you and sent you to his friend. And look at what happened. . It would have happened anyway, so it is true. It is easy to overlook the law but it is better to delight in the law of God. He prospers in all he does.

172.   The man of imagination trusts in the fulfillment of his wish and commits himself to it. For the art of fortune, he may be tempted to do the same.173. The sixth disciple is named Bartholomew. Bartholomew is the sixth disciple. Awakened imagination puts the person who is awakened above the rest, making him appear like a beacon in a world that is dark. Disciplined imagination is the most distinguishing quality that separates man and man. This is the separation between the wheat and the chaff. Our artists, scientists, inventors, and other people with vivid imaginations are the ones who have contributed most to society.

174.   The man of imagination can control life.

175.   Who is this being that bears our sins, infirmities and diseases? Christ! Our amazing human imagination! Your imagination is the one that causes you pain or deep sorrow when you're in pain. You can tell a friend that he's not feeling well or in great pain if he tells you. . Christ. . Your friend wouldn't believe that Christ is suffering because he believes Christ to be another person than he. Christ is the human imagination. The Bible will not make any sense until man realizes this.

176.   This level allows you to start right now and achieve any dream. Let me tell you, you will live the life you have always imagined. So imagine well. Imagine the most beautiful thing in the universe and imagine. . No matter how beautiful it may be. . It is nothing when compared to who you are. You are the only thing that this world can compare to. The world of Caesar is a small part of your infinite self, but you can still dream big. You can have beautiful dreams if you're willing to believe that you already have everything. Start to visualize yourself as the woman or man you desire to be. No matter what happens tomorrow, next week, next month, or the future, you will be that person in this world.Yes, everything here will disappear. . But why not try your creative powers? You will soon discover the power that lies within you and be able to conjure things out of your depth. You will discover the truth of your creativity power when you act boldly and persistently as if it were true.

177.   Remember that everything you see is not what you see. If you set goals, you don't have to worry about how others will react. You can see the money in you if you desire a lot of money. You can then claim it as yours!

178.   Tonight, you believe it even though everyone around you denies it. Your friends also deny it. And you dare to think that you are the man. . Already the man, already she . You are exactly where you want to be. As you believe that you are, you can walk in it as if it were true. You will find yourself leading the way to the realization of your assumption. No one can stop you if you persist in this belief. Believe that imagination creates reality."I tell you therefore, whatever you pray, believe that it will be granted to you." It's that simple. . But how do I believe that it is mine? If I believed that I had received something today, I might see the world differently. It wouldn't have been possible for me to see it before that realization. Mentally, I would look at the world as if I had become the man I desire to be. From that assumption I would be able to commune with my wife, my daughters, and my friends. Even though I am not physically compelled to, I should still believe it is true and continue that assumption.

If I do, I can tell you that I have experience and it will happen.

This is the highest level. It is true at the moment I believe it. That moment is the creative act. Man's memory is short, and he can't recall the act. So when he reaps the harvest, he denies it is his. He didn't plant it. Yet, there is a law that says everything will bear according its nature. It cannot produce anything other than its own nature.

179.   I encourage you to apply his teachings. He said to you that it was important to implyally appropriate a subjective state, which is your objective hope. It must also externalize itself in your life. It will happen if you do that. Be confident and ask in faith. Those who doubt are like the waves of the sea being tossed and driven by the wind. They are dual-minded because they know what they have and want to be another. It is important to be single-minded. You need to let go of what you think you are and assume that you are what you want. You will be able to see the amazing law of liberty that sets you free and your friends will also be able to see it. Keep believing in the possibility that it will happen.

180.   Your faith is the link between your imaginal act, and its fulfillment. It is simply your subjective appropriation or objective hope. Hoping your desire . . Subjectively adapted. . True, faith is your link towards objectivity.

181.   Only Christ has ever existed within you, as your unique human imagination.

182.   It is very simple: You will reap what you sow. It's the law that like breeds like. Your life will become what you visualize. Assume the feeling you would have if you had what you desire. You will achieve your dream if you persist in that feeling.

183.   You can believe what you want to become a reality by using the amazingcreative power of your imagination. In the first Psalm, we are told: "Blessed be the man who delights the law of God." He prospers in all he does. This law, which is explained in the Sermon on the Mount as psychological, is psychological. You have probably heard the old saying, "Thou shalt never commit adultery." But I'm here to tell you that anyone who lusts for a woman has committed adultery with her heart. It is not enough to stop the urge from the outside. Adultery begins the moment that the desire is felt!

184.   Many people believe that Man does not exist, but I say that Man is allImagination. Imagination is God.

185.   A creative act that is called an imaginal act is one that is creative. The seed (or state) of the imaginal act is fertilized when it is felt. It may take some time for it to become a reality. So, start today by pretending you are the man or woman you want to be. Let your imagination guide you to the truth. Keep your assumptions true. This thought is key to bringing your desires to fruition. Do not persist in fear or effort, but rather wait for your imaginal act to become a reality.

186.   There are many states and levels of consciousness in the Father's house. Choose one, then enter it and take control. Your Father is the good shepherd, and your needs are his sheep. The good shepherd gathers all your wishes for yourself and others and takes them to the field. How does this happen? It's all in your imagination. You can imagine! Your sheep will listen to your voice and follow you into the fold. The 10th chapter of John tells us that the good shepherd is the first to leave and the sheep will follow. Signs are not pre-ordained. They follow. Put yourself in the desired position to bring your desires into reality. Keep going until you experience it.You can imagine reality by imagining it. Thank your Father for this and then drop it. Do not try to change it. Only know that you have the power to create it. Expect a delay in your birth. There will always be intervals between conception and fulfillment. One seed might take 21 days, while another may take five months, nine or more months, and so on. It doesn't matter how long it takes for the seed to be fertilized and the hatching of its seeds. All that matters is knowing the seed of your desire has been planted in your mind. If your sheep wander off, you can bring them back to your flock when you are sure who the good shepherd is. If you don't know who the good shepherd is, there are many sheep-shepherds who will fleece your sheep!

187.   Man's inner conversation mirrors his imagination. His imagination is a government in which no opposition ever comes to power.

188.   Inner speaking reveals the activities and causes of life's circumstances.

189.   "The wise men, prophets, and kings of old would have givenanything for to have heard the things you have heard, and to have seen the things you've seen. But they didn't." So in our State Department. . or the Foreign Office of England or any other foreign office of any country in the world . They are not hearing the same thing as you. They don't understand this. They must be rational beings who play the same game they have played for centuries with all their mistakes and replaying the silly things over and over. It's not possible to forget because God doesn't forget and we create it by our imaginations.What are you imagining tonight? It doesn't matter what it is, one day you will be shocked beyond your wildest imaginations when you see the other side. As in the tale of Lazarus laughing, he returns from the dead with all the values changed. The rich were no longer poor and the poor weren't poor. Everything was reversed on that side, so all the values were changed. Lazarus also laughed at some of our actions. You should not forget God's laws. "Blessed" is the man who delights and prospers under the Lord's law.

190.   Jesus Christ is your amazing human imagination, and his story is all about you. It is told in third person. You feel like another is suffering, but you are the one suffering. You will not be able to see God if you don't believe you are God unless you do.

191. You don't need to say what you want, you can simply assume itIt is yours, and you can use it for. . Although your rational mind and outer senses may deny it. . If you believe in yourself, your desires will be realized. Your power of belief is unlimited and anything is possible for anyone who believes. Imagine what an incredible power that is. It doesn't matter if you are smart, kind, or good. Anything is possible if you believe what you imagine is true. This is how you will achieve success.

192.   Imagine the mystery of creation as a story. Then, keep faith in the unrevealed reality of what already exists.

193.   The Book of Luke tells the story of a man who arrived at a house at midnight and said, "A friend has come who is hungry." I would like to have three loaves bread. The man upstairs said: "It's midnight. The man upstairs replied: "It is midnight. My children are asleep in bed and I can't come down to give you what your want." This statement is then made: "But due to the man's importunity, he received all that he wanted." "Brazen impudence" is the definition of "importunity". A man who has a desire will not accept no as an answer. You don't have to ask God for what you want. Instead, ask yourself how you can bring it about!God is. . Your own amazing human imagination. . You will answer when you refuse to take no for an explanation. Your denial comes from within, and there is no other source. You are the only one who can insist on believing you have what you want. Even though it was past midnight, the father decided to give what was necessary, even though the rest of the family was sleeping. As there is only one human imagination, the God of a Blake or Einstein does not differ from your God. There can't be two Gods. He is not a dual God. Your imagination and you are no less than anyone else, but you have to learn persistence.

194.   Christ is your wonderful human imagination, and all things. All things, good or bad, are equally important. . You can even imagine the unloveliest things you want and then perpetuate them. False statements like Christ only makes good, and the devil only makes evil are false. If you have doubts about the power of Christ within you . That's the devil. If you don't believe "I AM" to be the being you seek, and instead pray to him using your human imagination, then you won't reach your goal. Awareness is the only power that can grant it to you. imagination.

195.   You are not a prisoner of anyone or anything, but you have been imprisoned. All of your experiences have been created by you and you can alter them once you understand who you are. Don't think about another person when you hear the Lord. Yod Hey Vav Hey is the word that means "I AM", as well as Father and potter. Your awareness of yourself is your I AM, the potter who shapes your world. All of your responsibilities for the world you create are up to him and him only. Your amazing human imagination is what restricts the freedom you have today.There is no other cause than the Lord, who is also the Father and the potter. If he is your amazing human imagination, then who can you praise or blame for your current circumstances? Blind leaders of the blind blame society and the government for their lives. You will find no other cause, for you are the only one responsible. You are the only one responsible for society, government, family, and friends. They may seem to have been pushed aside, but there are many things that still exist within you. Divine Imagination (the Lord God Almighty), has reproduced Himself in your. . The human imagination, and the Divine Imagination includes all things within Himself.

196.   You will create in your outer world what you see in your mind's eye. It's that simple. I hope that you can see your fulfilled desires in your mind's eyes. Scripture tells us that you will be what you believe you are if you are self-persuaded.

197.   You can test God, and if He passes the test then you will discover that God is just a human imagination. You can put God to the test by believing that the one you are looking for is available now. It will happen if you keep believing that it will. Don't worry about when or how it will happen. Just assume it has already happened and you will be able to identify God when it happens.

198.   Remember that a storm can only be raging because of your inattention to your imagination. You can wake up from the sleep of inadequacy and be aware of the things you desire to see by disciplining your thoughts. You will see the world change and adapt to your ideas. The storm will end and the world will become calm again. You are God's temple and the spirit of God lives in you. Ask most people where they think God's temple is located. Most will point out a church, synagogue or cathedral. But God doesn't dwell in homes made with hands. God is spirit, and he dwells in his living temple. Think about it. . God is working. Be confident in the reality that you're imagining. Adjust the little clusters that are around your foot. Once they feel good, you can relax knowing that the outside world will follow the new arrangement. The world may appear external but its reality is inside. You are the creative power that dreams the world into existence. You will one day wake up from this dream and discover that you have experienced the mystery of dying.

199.   It doesn't matter how it will happen. Your imagination will do the rest. "I am the beginning and the ending." "My ways have been discovered." Your imagination is an instantaneous creative act. In this three-dimensional world events occur in a sequence. Your inner conversations should be in line with your imagination. You have already planted a seed, and you will soon reap the rewards.

200.   You can solve any situation with the right use of imagination.QUOTES 201- 300

201.   Based on my personal experiences, I believe that the God of the Bible is our wonderful human imagination. That God and the human imagination are one, that all natural effects in the universe, even if they are created by God's Spirit, are caused by Spirit. Every natural effect has a spiritual cause and is not natural. It is not a natural cause that appears; it is a delusion from our." . Fading, I would call it "memory". (Blake, taken from "Milton") Because I don't remember exactly when I imagined what is happening in my world right now. It is not something I can recall. It is not clear when it was set in the notion. If this is Law, . A Law that can't be broken by man, . At some point, I thought of what I was seeing now. It isn't receding into my past, it is moving into the future to confront and confront me. But I didn't remember it.
It does not appear to have a natural or physiological cause.Or, the Bible is totally wrong. "Every natural effect has an spiritual cause" We are told that "By Him all things were created." . Without exception, "and without Him, nothing was made that was made." It is only at this level that I don't recall having imagined it. But, somewhere along the way, I might have, if this was Principle.

202.   The key to scripture is I AM. Jesus Christ is the NewTestament's name for God the Father. His name is known in the Old Testament as "I AM" and it is called Jesus Christ. You cannot return empty-handed having come into this world to fulfill the word. You inspired the prophets to tell you your story. This was not just to fulfill their prophecy but also to inspire others.

203.   One man I saw in New York City during World War II claimed to have despised Roosevelt. The man would talk to himself every morning in the mirror and tell Roosevelt all he hated about him. When I confronted him about his fantasies, he stated that he would not pay $10 for a Broadway show that gave him the joy he gets during those ten minutes. This man was a scheming tyrant, and the venom he spew every morning was his own storm. After he had lost his New York City house, he moved to Florida where he eventually lost all of his possessions. I tried to get him to wake up, but he was only dreaming Roosevelt was his cause. He refused to believe me. He was from Germany and couldn't believe that we were at war.Even though he knew that Germany had declared war against us, he blamed Roosevelt. He couldn't see the war as a bad nightmare, and he was making it worse by blaming Roosevelt for his pleasure in telling Roosevelt off while he shaved. You can think what you want. You can increase your hatred by being persistent and intense. It is the same if you love someone. For your human imagination, he is the only God that you will ever see. . That temple is yours!

204. All that has been constructed up by natural religion is thrown into the fires of mental fire. . Knowing that every time you use your imagination to help another person, you are actually mediating God to men and thereby feeding and clothing Christ Jesus. And that any time you think evil against another person, you are literally beating Christ Jesus?

205.   This is the story of a man who learned not to look for help from anyone outside. All help came from within. He was a young boy from a poor Russian family. He was eight years old when he started running errands in order to make money to feed his family. He had never been to a restaurant, bought a shirt, slacks or shoes before and was well aware of the horrors associated with minority groups. His family is Jewish. The job required him to take large sums of money to the bank to exchange them for small denominations. He noticed that the copper coins of the teller resembled those of the silver ones. As he gave the money back to his employer, he started to play with himself. He imagined the riches he would have if the teller had given his silver coins instead of his copper. The teller made the same mistake the next day. The young man gave him silver rather than copper. He then took the money to another bank to change it into the correct

denomination. When he returned to work, he gave his employers what they wanted.The boy was taught right and wrong and he fought his conscience all night. But in the morning, he took the money and bought new shoes, a shirt, and pants. He then went to a restaurant to enjoy his meal to the fullest. He didn't return the money but learned a valuable lesson. After hearing his story, the world would think he was crazy. But when we came out of the Father, we ate from the tree of good or evil. And there isn't one person on this planet who hasn't violated that code. Although he may not be able to offend the moral code, the drama of life can still be seen as psychological.

The child was hungry. He was hungry. He has returned to society ten times more than the little he took, not because of the lessons learned. He came to Paris as a street-cleaner after Russia's collapse in the First World War. He remembered his past and began to remember what it was like. Today, he is a multimillionaire and owns a legitimate business.

206.   When I visited my family in Barbados, I was told that I couldn't leave Barbados for seven months. But I wanted to go on the next boat. I felt that being on that boat was the end of my life. . While sitting in a chair at my parent's house. . I imagined myself entering the boat and looking at the island as I went. Although I didn't know how I would get there, I found out a week later that the boat had left the island. This is what I have learned from personal experience. You must have an imagination to travel anywhere. Even those who might not agree with your request will help you when it is time. That's how I got out the army. I knew I wanted to be discharged with honor and so I slept in my New York City apartment as if it had already occurred. My captain then. . who had previously disallowed me from being discharged. . I had a change in heart, which led to my release. It is possible for anyone to do it.This is a simple game that can be a lot of fun. Imagine a thing you'd like to have. Imagine a place that you would like to live in. Next, find an object in the room and feel it until you can sense its vividness. It shouldn't be a lamp but that lamp. And it shouldn't be a table but that table. You can feel the chair all around you by sitting in that chair. You can see the entire room from this chair. Feel the relief from being there and put your bread on the water. Then, let your genie go. . Who is your slave? . You will build a bridge of incidents over which you will cross to reach that chair, touch the table, and hold that lamp.

207.   Learn how to tune your imagination tonight. Tune in to your friend's voice. Listen carefully and determine the words that you want him to use. Listen to him until he speaks clearly. Then, believe that you have heard him. It really did happen. It will happen if you want it to. It is impossible to say when, as every imaginal act can be compared to an egg. No two eggs, unless they are the same species, have the same time period for hatching. A little bird emerges in three weeks, a small sheep in five months, a horse takes twelve months and a human in nine. Your imaginal act will ripen and blossom at its own time. It may seem long so wait. . It is certain and it will not be late.

208.   God is still within each individual man until he believes in his wonderful humanimagination. It is because you don't believe that you can harvest God's promises!

209.   Sometimes it may take you a thousand times before you convince yourself that things are what they should be. The outer world will reflect your inner harmony only if you can be convinced that you have achieved it. One of our greatest educators is William James, Harvard's professor of psychology. He stated, "The greatest revelation of my generation is that human beings can make outer changes in harmony to their inner convictions by changing their inner attitude."

210.   Your amazing human imagination is God's creative power. It is your salvation. Water is your savior if you are thirsty. Employment is your salvation if you are in dire need of work. You have the power to rescue yourself from any situation. Your imagination can help you achieve your heart's desires. Your imagination can do anything. You are only limited by your imagination. You can do anything you imagine.

211.   Any faith in any power that is not He (imagination) is false, and anyone who teaches power from the outside is a fake teacher. Christ (imagination in you) is your hope for glory. There is no other power.

212.   Keep dreaming up the things you desire until you achieve them. To achieve your desires, you need to do nothing more. You will be guided to take the necessary action if it is necessary. It is not necessary to "help" bring about the change. It is God who does the work, and He knows how to do it. When you think about your wish during the day, be thankful that it is already a reality. . Because it is!

213.   Your creative potential is limitless. If you can think of a solution to the most terrible problem, it will be solved. It is possible for anyone to do it. You don't need to be Einstein to see a solution. Don't limit your creativity by trying to determine the best way for it to happen. Your imagination has many possibilities that you don't know about. Don't worry about where, how, and when. . The end is not the beginning. What is the solution if you are in debt? What if you win the lottery? Or your uncle dies leaving you his fortune? No! You are debt-free at the end. What would it feel like to have all your bills paid? Let imagination make that feeling a reality!

214.   There is a solution to every problem. Assume the solution is true. How would it make you feel if true? What would it feel like? Keep that feeling going and you will find the solution. God can do anything, and God has been crucified on your behalf as your amazing human imagination. All things are possible for him. There has never been another God. Imagine the end and you will be able to imagine all possible outcomes. If you believe that it is possible, your imagination will become a reality.Creative power does not exist by itself. It is not enough to know what to do. Your imagination's operant power must allow you to believe that everything is as you want them to be before it can come to pass. What is the time it takes for a state of being objective? It will take as long as it takes for the seed to germinate. You are only required to enter the state and stay there psychologically. While you'll still be physically present on the planet as one person, when you think from your preferred psychological state, it takes on physical dimensions and becomes a reality in your world.

215.   Now, I realize that I am the center of my creative power. You will one day awaken and use your creative power knowingly. This is our destiny. We all will become Gods and be able to use the power of creation in the truest sense. Remember that God has unlimited creative power and your belief power. You can convince yourself that everything is as you want them to be. As a sign of faith, you can fall asleep in this assumption. Tomorrow, the world will change to make way for your assumed garment.They will arrive, regardless of whether it takes one or ten thousand people to help you assume. Their consent or permission is not required. The world is already dead, so why would you ask dead people for help? Just know what you want and animate it. The actors will move toward the fulfillment of your desires. Before you judge it, try it. It may not make sense but it will be proven in performance, and it will no longer matter what the rest of the world thinks. Does it really matter what another person thinks about a thing if there is proof for it? You can't fail if you try it.

216.   Start now to believe in God, your true Being, and believe that whatever you imagine is true, it will be true.

217.   You know what you want. Close your eyes and you will find it. It is that He hears what you say; and God (consciousness), externalizes what He sees, hears, and remains loyal.

218.   Here's the story. He stated, "Unless you are born again, you cannot enter the kingdom of Heaven." The wise man replied, "How is it possible that a man my own age may once more enter my mother's womb to be born again?" He replied, "You are a master of Israel, and you don't know?" You cannot enter the kingdom of Heaven unless you are born from water and the spirit. He then gives us this hint: "As Moses lifted the serpent in wilderness, so must the son or man be lifted."...as Moses lifted the serpent...do you think that a man lifted a brazen serpent, as described in the story, and that everyone who saw it was immediately healed? It is not a serpent. The serpent symbolises the power of self-replication endlessly. The serpent is a symbol of the power of endless self-reproduction. It sheds its skin but does not die. Man must be like the serpent who grows and outgrows. Therefore, I need to learn how to die so that I can live. I die by laying down everything I have.

Now I believe and I feel empowered to believe that I can be what I want. This is how I get it done.

219.   You are asked to use your creativity every day. Living with absolute faith in Jesus Christ (your own Wonderful Human Imagination) is a must. Because you are a human, he is a person. The creative power of the universe will make a state you have imagined possible. Claim aYou can create a glorious future for your self by making the present the past. Your friends should congratulate and congratulate your success now. Have faith in Jesus Christ knowing that he is your Wonderful Human Imagination!

220.   You are God, the only actor of this world. God acts no matter what you imagine. God is the only actor who acts by imagining. It is possible to imagine anything. If you believe in the possibility, it will happen.

221.   You can test God if you wish. You don't need to be awake to see the creative potential of your immortal eyes and ears. Assume that you are the person you desire to be. You will be able to believe it even if everything around you denies it. It doesn't matter who you are, or what the world thinks about you. Anything is possible for the "I" of imagination.

222.   You will find that your creativity is tested on this level. Believe that you can be the man or woman you desire to become. Feel the sense that you are already there. This assumption will help you see your world and realize its truth. Believe that your assumption will blossom at its own time. Keep believing in your belief until it becomes a fact. This is Christianity!

223.   This principle was new to me when I discovered it. I was skeptical at first. I don't know how anyone could believe that a thing is possible without having any evidence. How can any imaginal act, which projects and fuses itself, be the causative factor? Even though I didn't believe it could, my imagination led me to what I didn't want. Let me now share what I know about the principle of imagining, and guide you to your decision and its risk. There is always risk. You might not like what you imagined.

224.   Take a mental picture of your world. While your present level of objective reality may be the same as before, you can imagine your friends congratulating you on your good fortune. Believe in this unreality. As Paul said, don't look at things seen but things unseen. The things seen are temporary, while the unseen are eternal.

225.   This level is where the dream of life unfolds. We don't know the hidden causes of these events and can't see them. It is all in our imagination. All things are not derived from the obvious causes they are attributed to, but from something else. . The amazing human imagination is all man can dream up! The April issue of Atlantic Monthly contains an article by General   David M. Shoop (retired commandant of Marine Corps). He claims that there are a few high-ranking officers in this country who want to make this nation a militaristic, aggressive nation.They believe that war will lead to the promotion and glory they seek. This is something they cannot do while in peacetime. They dream of a war that they can command in glory. Where? The hidden cause of all existence is in their amazing human imagination! You can use imagination infernally. . As these men do. . Or towards the kingdom of Heaven. You can do this by thinking about a friend and listening to him share his good news. As he speaks, you can see his expressions change. As he stands tall in clothes he loves, you can feel the excitement of his transformation. If you believe what you see is real, then you can rest assured that your friend will one day conform to your imagination!

226.   All things are created by imagination. Everything disappears where there is no imagination. If there is lack in your world now, and you stop being aware of it by visualizing plenty, then lack vanishes. Therefore, any modification to your belief system will result in a positive change in your life.

227.   Are you clear about what you want in life? If you know who and what you are, you can become anything you want. For eternity (all things), start with the premise that "I AM all imagination" and move through states. Although you might think that a state is gone after you have lived in it, all states remain eternal and will never cease to exist. You can move between states unknowingly or wittingly, but your personal identity remains the same forever, just like the mental traveler you are. No matter how rich or poor you may be, your individual identity is the same regardless of whether you move between states. You can easily be persuaded, whether by television, radio or the press, to alter your self-concept and move unknowingly into a less desirable state. While you can be an actor in many different states, your identity will not change. You are the same actor whether you're rich or poor. These are just different roles you play.

228.   Purposive living can be achieved by focusing your imagination on theaction and feeling fulfilled desire. This awareness and sensitiveness will allow you to initiate and feel movement in the inner world.

229.   You must create an action in your imagination to realize your desires. This is independent of any evidence from the senses.

230.   The mind created the world out of unseen things and gave life by faith. Eternity exists, and all things exist in eternity, independent from the creative act which is the assumption and loyalty to the assemblage. Even if your senses or reason deny it, if you are faithful to the unseen assumption, it will externalize. This is how all worlds are created, but men don't understand it. They continue to create the world they don't want by structuring it based on their senses.

231.	This is the basis of imagining reality. This is my premise. Don't believe that you can think idly about the record. So, just as a man plants, so too will he reap. It is rare for anything in the world to happen by chance. However, you can't recall the exact moment when it happened. It is impossible to relate the natural effect to it. The natural effect has always had a spiritual cause, and not a natural one. It is only a illusion. It's a delusion. Don't believe anyone who says you can track it back to a physical cause. It is not a cause. It is only an effect. All causes are spiritual, and I don't mean the imaginal. Because man is all imagination, and God is also man, and He exists in us and in us. The imagination is the eternal body of man, and God is that. God is the only source. There is no other source. It ends on a beautiful note in the 87th Psalm, which I quoted tonight. "And both the singers as well as the dancers said, You are our springs." There is no other spring, source or cause. You can be the greatest singer or dancer in the world. Your springs are yours. There is no other source.

232.	The moment that he senses the presence of another person in him, man awakens to his imaginative life.

233.	Create a mental drama that implies your desire is realized. Immobilize your outer self and act exactly as if you were going to sleep. Then, start the predetermined action in your imagination.

234.	Every natural effect has a spiritual reason. Naturalcauses only seem. It is a delusion of vegetable memory, perishing. These moments in time are not recalled. When that imaginal state is created so that we can see it with our outer eyes, we don't recognize our harvest and deny having any influence on the natural effects taking place in our world. We don't remember because our memory is defective.

235.   Your imagination is your only limit. It is your reality and you can't escape it. This is the truth. It suffers alongside you. You are the Lord Jesus Christ. Tonight, test Him. You can test Him for the good. Are you looking for a better job? Don't listen to what the papers tell you. You don't need to believe everything you read. "All things are possible for the Lord Jesus Christ." (Matthew 19,26). If you don't have enough money, ignore what the paper says. You assume you have it. God does not limit the power to believe. Can you believe it? Try it.First, believe in God. God is only your imagination. Believe in Him, that anything you can think of is possible. Imagine that you could have the job you desire. Imagine the income it would bring. What about the enjoyment of doing the work? Then, walk as if it were true. Even though your senses may deny it, the world will say it's false. But if you keep believing it, it will become a fact. This is the law that your wonderful imagery makes possible. It is possible to believe it and make it a reality.

236.   The man of imagination lives in the end, certain that he will also live there in flesh.

237.   All causation comes from man, and only that is man's amazing human imagination. It is important to take this into consideration and you will never forget it. It's impossible to blame anyone else in the world for what happens. There's no one you can blame for anything that happens in this world. Do not let anyone say this to you. Do not listen to them. They're simply bringing it into the world through what they see morning, noon and night. If one is able to visualize unlovely aspects of another person, or unlovely aspects of a group, they will simply create it. They will not find it in the group but within themselves.

238.   I will give you water, explaining how the law works. You must now turn it into wine through application. You are not allowed to continue drinking water. According to the Book of Timothy, you are instructed to drink no more water but to have a glass of wine for your stomach and any other ailments. It's great to know what to do, but we have the operant power. We must not only know what to do, but also do it. When I do it, I stop drinking water and start drinking wine. Because I start to apply it, it's wine. If I don't know   how to apply it but have no idea what it is, then I have water, but not wine. Let's all practice this and make it a daily habit. It will not fail you, let me assure you. It will not fail you.

239.   The first act of creativity recorded in scripture is the time when the spiritofthe Lord moved uponthe surface of the water. This is motion. You can go anywhere you want to by closing your eyes to the current room and imagining a different place. Your senses will refuse to perceive any change. It was only a psychological action. The obvious here disappears when you close your eyes. Assumption makes it possible to create the here. You create reality by seeing the world in relation to your new position. Although this may seem absurd, Douglas stated that "The secret to imagining is one of the greatest problems." The solution to this mystery will bring you supreme power, supreme wisdom and supreme delight. How can this mystery be solved? You can claim that you are only imagination. Next, wrap yourself in space and mentally see your world relative to that assumed place in space. That's it! You have moved.240

It is only the name that people give to those who do not know the power and function imagination has on the works of imagination.

241.As your Human Imagination, test Jesus Christ, God's creative power within you! Are you looking for a better job? Do you want more money? You can claim it as easily as I did the rose. Wear it like it's true, and feel the possession. What if it's a better job? Where would you be seated if it was yours? What would your mate think of you? Let your husband or wife see you from behind the special desk. Believe in Jesus Christ and live as if it were true.

242.I slept in my father's house in my imagination like I was there in flesh. I felt compelled to also experience the same state in flesh by fusing my imagination with the state.

243.	The Word of God, also known as the HumanImagination, created the world!

244.	Jesus Christ is the one who created all things in this world, good and bad. Who is He? Your amazing Human Imagination! God's creative power . as pure imagining . . He is in your soul at the root of all your faculties, including perception. He is most often hidden in the form creative fancy, but he flows into your surface mind.

245.	A new state can be entered by imagining oneself in the feeling of a fulfilled wish.

246.	What are you thinking right now? It could be something terrible. Is it a terrible thought? Whatever your thoughts, they will be realized, because there is no other world than the one you first imagined.

247.   We all have the power to imagine our destiny, good or bad. The power of imagination is unlimited and can be used to achieve objective realization. Every stage of man's progression or fall is possible through the use of imagination. William Blake said, "What appears to be, is, for those who believe it to be." I agree with him. It can produce the most terrible consequences to those who believe it to be, including torment, despair, and death. We can become what we want to be by using imagination and our desire. We are exactly what we think we are. We will transform into the person we imagine ourselves to be if we continue to believe that we can be what we want to be.Our lives were made possible by the natural miracle of love. For a short time, our needs were taken care of by another. This simple truth is the key to life. We cannot live without love. In their own ways, our parents cannot transmit life. We can see that love is the only way to create life. Therefore, no love, no life. It is therefore rational to conclude that "God is Love."

248.   God's creative power is buried within you. Your spiritual birth is God's creative power. Your imagination is the spirit that you have buried within yourself. God. . being spirit . . He has placed his seed, which will erupt in one day. You will experience a spiritual birth.

249.   Neville, a physical man, can't do anything. But I can imagine doing everything! Imagine a thing, and then think it will happen. This is like saying amen, believing that it will happen because it was imagined. It is impossible to predict how it will come about. It will happen, I know that.

250. You can turn to the only God, your wonderful Human.Imagination! Learn to adore him. God can do all things, so it is possible to imagine anything! If you know what you want, you can ask yourself whether you believe your imaginal acts were committed by God. They are, I swear!

251.   Now, I want you to think about yourself. Do you look to the outside when faced with a problem? Or do you believe all power is within your own imagination? Are you a believer in the hydrogen bomb, the right people or the "right" side? Do you believe in the power of your imagination? Jesus of Nazareth is the one I believe in. He is the author of Moses and the law. I look to him for solutions to my problems. It is by asking myself what I would imagine if my problem was solved. What would you hear? What would you say?After discovering Jesus to be my imagination, it is easy to act as if the problem has been solved. I have also found that I can bring things into the world that are not visible to the mortal eye. It works and I encourage you to do it. You can examine yourself and make sure that you are sure that Jesus Christ is your only Savior. You have failed the test if you look to anyone other than yourself. Only turn to God, and not to anyone or anything outside. Your future cannot be predicted by anyone, because your future is to live up to Scripture!

252.   Passive surrender to the appearances and bow before evidence is to admit that Christ (Imagination), is not yet born in your heart.

253.   Reason is limited by its nature to the evidence of the senses. However, imagination, which has no such limitation can satisfy our needs.

254.   People are unaware of the incredible power of theimagination. But once he begins to recognize this power, he stops playing the same role he played before. He does not turn around and become a mere reflector of the world; he becomes the effector of it all. It is important to keep your imagination focused on the feeling of fulfillment and not lose sight of that. Our ability to live in the fulfillment of our wishes is what allows us to live a more fulfilling life. Many of us fear that we will be seen as noble and important individuals who can make a positive contribution to the world. However, our senses and reason are able to disprove our assumptions. It seems like we are in the grips of an unconscious urge that makes us hold on to our familiar world and resist any threat to shake us from it.

255.   Only one creator exists. The Human Imagination is the one who creates, kills, wounds, and heals. It doesn't matter if you misuse or use your creative power. The same being will bring it about. If you want beautiful things, imagine wonderful thoughts. Your friends are your limitations and lacks made visible. Pray for your friends, just like Job. Your fears will be lifted.

256.   Humanity is the only place that can hold the creative power of all things. It is the same creative power that exists in everyone. God allows you to misuse Christ (Imagination), His creative power. In the end, He will awaken you and all violence in you will cease. You will be infinitely loved, infinitely wise, and infinitely powerful. You will then see that the shadows of the world are gone and there will be no need to fight them.

257.   If you believe that all things are possible, and that you can imagine them all, then you should be able accomplish any task and satisfy every wish. First, you have to be open to the possibility that you can do anything. You can decide what you believe. Are you a mortal man? . Or all imagination?

258.   This is Neville, the "outer man", who first came into the world. Then, there is another. . My own amazing human imagination. This is the "Jacob" that enters the world. They are not two different little boys. This is the story. It is an adumbration to that which is later in the New Testament. That the One who could say "I AM FROM ABOVE and YOU ARE FROM DOWN; you are of the world, I am not of the world," is what is being spoken of. And the "thing below," is the body you are "wearing," which is "of the world."We

are dealing with the greatest mystery in the universe, the mystery of imagination. Fawcett stated that "The secret to imagining is one of the most difficult problems in the world, and the solution to which all men should strive, for supreme power. supreme wisdom. supreme delight lie within the far-off solution to this mystery." . Because you are solving the problem God! You can solve the problem by imagining!

259. It is difficult for man to identify himself with his imagination. But the word "logos" helps. . Translated "Word" is "a purpose; plan; a pattern.".Divine Imagination is the Word that was with God at the beginning. It is through this that all things are created. It is impossible to find a single thing in the modern world that was not originally imagined. Although you may not be able to grasp the concept of nature being first imagined, you can't deny that clothing, transportation, and business were all imagined.

260.   Happiness is dependent on our ability to use imagination to inwardly and actively affirm that we are who we want to be.

261.   Tonight, I challenge you to use your human imagination. Your friends are just you out pictured. Make sure to show them a shining light. You can't justify their actions by saying "It serves them well", since all things are within you. There is only one you, and there is no one else. If you fail thousand times, you will ask: "How many times Lord must I forgive my brother who sinned against moi?" The answer will be: "Seventy times seven."Who is this being in which I have sinned against? His name is I AM! How could I have sinned against you and thee? Allowing someone in my world who is in greatest need to continue their stay, because I cannot sin against another person as I

I am the one who sees it. Therefore, I must make him see me as the person I want to be. That belief must be maintained until he accepts the image that I have created. This is what you're called to do. You were made to be vanity and you live alone in your world. If you want it to change, it is up to you to make it change and live in that state.

This is something I have experienced. The night I was lifted to perfection, I saw this endless sea of human imperfections. As I glided past, all seemed to be in perfect harmony with the state I had been lifted to. You must strive to be the world you want it to be, for everything is you made visible. All of the world projects God and God is I AM! Trust my visions. They have never betrayed. Although I might betray my vision and refuse to accept its message, I was lifted up and shown that every person I meet is me. If I make him appear different to me, the more I hold on to that assumption, the more he will conform to my expectations.

262.   The power of imagination can bring things to life, but it can also take them away! It can also uncreate what it creates. We have created nightmares in this beautiful world that we can't endure forever. They will need to be erased. It is for this reason that I encourage everyone to live a noble life. You must plant ideas that are worthy of remembering. Because the day will come when anything built on other foundations than imagination will either be destroyed or created. All kinds of bad things are brought into our world, and we live with them until they disappear. You can create or uncreate. If you have brought something that you don't love into your life, you can create something new.

263.   Each stage in man's development is achieved by his conscious use of his imagination to match his inner speech and fulfill his desires.

264.   My imagination seems to have two sides. Neville and my imagination. Although imagination is not visible, I am certain that I cannot separate from it. My creative power cannot be separated from me. My imagination is my very existence. Although I can talk about my imagination, I cannot separate myself completely from it. Divine Imagination is God's creative force that creates and sustains the universe. If God were to change his imagination, the world would end. It is necessary for it to exist. It is the same in your world. You can only change it if you stop dwelling in your current imaginal state!

265.   There is no one who owes me anything. All I have to do it trust Jesus Christ and my human imagination. I don't have the desire to accumulate a lot of money. Why accumulate a million shadows when you can have a million? My goal is to show you Jesus Christ. He is your amazing human imagination. There has never been another Christ, and there will never be another. You can trust him. . I use the term "him" with caution because God's creative power is in you, and God is a person. . You will never fail because he will never leave you behind! If you are certain of what you want tonight, you can just believe it. As if it were true, sleep as though it was. Christ, your own human imagination is within everyone. He will use all the necessary resources to help you become your assumption.

266.   We can live in infinite states but our body of belief is the fundamental state we are operating from. Your thoughts will flow from the belief that you are limited. If this principle holds true, then you can modify that belief to make it more effective. Your outer world will always reflect your inner thoughts. All you are is your imagination.

267.   Man can escape the limitations of his senses and the bonds of reason by using imagination.

268.   This world is real even though it appears very real. It is only a vision. "All that you see, even though it appears outside, is inside, in your Imagination, of which the world of mortality is only a shadow." If God is life, and God is your imagination then everything that the world calls life is just an activity of your imagination. You can stop creating and take control of what seems animated and independent from your perception. You will then know Christ, because you will discover that "In him is Life" and "His life is the Light of Men." God is the one who animates man within himself. Although it appears that humanity is independent and has their own life, this is only an illusion. I am the one who creates them.AM!

269.   John, in his 14th chapter, tells us that imagination is his spirit-of-life. He says: "You believe God?" Believe in me also. Can you imagine your dreams coming true? You can believe that your desires are real and you can live like it is. Imagine if you can. . And imagination can create reality. . You will soon see the manifestation of your desires in your life. If it doesn't, you have proven that the principle is false. The principle is true, I assure you. . Your belief is the most important! There are no limits to your belief power or the results that belief can achieve. You will receive it no matter what you want. Are you able to believe that God is the only true God?

270.   It's a great idea, and I urge you to give it a try. You will be amazed at the great wisdom of the ancients if you give it a try. They told us it in their unique, amazing, and symbolical way. Unfortunately, you and I have misinterpreted their stories and taken it for history. They intended it to be an instruction to help us achieve our goals. The world of states is all around us, and imagination allows us to see it inwardly. These states exist, they are here now, but they remain only possibilities while we think OF them. They become overwhelmingly real when we think FROM and dwell in them. There is a big difference between thinking FROM and thinking OF the things you want in this world.271. Every state exists as a "mere possibility" if you think about it, but becomes overwhelming real when you think aboutit. The way of Christ (Imagination) is to think from the end.

272.   Our imagination connects with the state we desire.

273.   The Spirit will guide you into a room. You will be able to sense intuitively who and what power you feel, and you will stop any activity in your body. Everything will cease to move. It will all be dead when you look at that which seemed so alive but was not dependent on your perceptions. Once you let go of their activity, everything will reanimate and carry on its purpose. If the bird was flying when it was arrested, it will fly again when it is released. When someone is carrying food to a restaurant, . Although they can be kept in this position as long as they wish, . When you let go of the power that you believe you have, they will continue to serve you the meal as though nothing has happened.Is it possible to imagine doing this? It is true, I assure you. But as long as your identity is with the body of death and you believe it to be you, you won't realize that you are your own chance at glory. You are dead if you don't take care of your body and make it well. . The awareness that entered it. . I am a living being who will experience scripture in this dead body. When I was born, I took on the body of a slave. I am now a human being, and I will obey death until death, even death on the cross of Christ. In this state, I'll experience the word that I inspired the prophets, which is I AM God in you!

274.   You will be most stimulated by my words. They are practical and practical. You will find the Bible far more fascinating than any other book or article you've read. The Bible contains words that are as powerful and practical as anything else you've ever heard. The divine plan for ending the world is beyond all plots and plans of men. The Divine Imagination's goal is to reproduce Himself in human imagination, because God is only being born. There is only one imagination: the divine and human imagination. They are not different in intensity.It is possible to make any wish come true. I came that you might have life and have more of it. You will no longer be a slave to the universe or fearful of it. Instead, you will realize that you are one in God's creation. You will be able to ask for instantaneous answers and get them back. When you receive the full revelation of all I have said to you, all this will be yours.

275.   You must believe that there is only one cause. It is the HumanImagination. Everyone must and will do their part in bringing about a change in your beliefs. Someone who was once an enemy will now be a friend. You can dream nobly! You will remember the wonderful things that you love, and they will be in your future.

276.   If there is one cause, the storm's originator is the one who quenched the wind and sea. There can't be another. You can resolve any confusion in your life by using your imagination. The world will witness what you do. . You caused the change. Since there is no other cause, did you not also cause the confusion? Only one God and Father is all that exists. He is the only God who is above all. He is in every being. If He is present in all beings who say I AM, and there can only be one God, then no one can accuse the other; God's name, however, is not he, but I AM. It doesn't matter how it looks on the outside, I am its cause. Accept full responsibility for what you see. If you don't like what you see, you can change it. You will see the changes you have made when you exercise this power. You are free if you are willing to take on that responsibility.

277.   Everybody imagines! Are you able to believe that Christ, the power of imagination, is within you? If you believe so, God is in your life! If God is in your life, then you can't lose Him. All must be saved. God will save everyone. . The savior of every person. . is reconciling himself and bringing the individual awareness of those in whom He is buried into the kingdom with them.

278.   Tonight, I will share a principle with you: God is the greatest artist who. . Your own wonderful, human imagination. . is perfecting his craft through the ages, in the creation of his own image within you. Have you ever seen an image? Name it. Are you ready to assume you already have it and then wait for its objectification. Each image has its own time to mature and bloom. It doesn't matter how long it takes, because it will eventually arrive. Do you want to wait to find the happiness that you desire or do you prefer to look outside to make it happen? You will be a successful doctor, businessman, minister or any other position you choose if you apply this principle and allow it to happen.You can only imagine your dream and make it a reality by living your life as if it were a fact. God is your only enemy. Only God is greater than man. . This is a mistake. . Creates opposition and calls them Satan or the Devil, which are both just as nonexistent as St. Christopher. Millions believe they are real and give them power that they don't have. I encourage you to believe only in God, who is your amazing human imagination.

279.   The gateway to reality is imagination.

280.   Start now to practice the art and skill of imagining every single day. Concertpianists must practice constantly. If he doesn't practice, he won't be able to perform a concert. It is important to practice the art and skill of imagination every day, so that you can face a problem head-on.

281.   You must first assume that it is a dream if you want to replace what you currently have. It will become a dream when it becomes real. The creative power of imagination can create that which was not there, to be. It can also cause the unreal. This power is God.

282.   Let's now return to the interpretation of scripture. As allimagination, you can take any passage and place yourself in the center of the book. Do not think of a man who lived 2,000 centuries ago. Christ is your hope for glory. This is the Christ about whom the scriptures talk. As you read the story about Sarah and Abraham, enter the state of Abraham. Next, become Sarah when Sarah is at the center and Rebecca when Rebecca appears. The Book is written about you! This will give you the key to unlocking the most difficult passages in scripture. Don't give up. You will see the beauty in each story and you'll be able to see it clearly.

283.   All things were created through imagination, and nothing was possible without awareness.

284.   You can't say "I will have it someday" if you really want something. This is delaying your hopes and making your heart sick. If you believe that imagination creates reality, then you will set up a stage and paint beautiful scenes. You will then let them weave together so that the scenery comes back into your head and the actors can speak the words you have commanded.

285.   Being and believing are one. Both the conceiver as well as his conception are one. The conceiver and his conception are one. Therefore, the conceiver can never be as far away from what you imagine yourself to be than it is to be close to him. Because nearness implies separation. "All things are possible for those who believe if they believe." Faith is the substance and evidence of what we have yet to see. You will be able to see other people as if you believe you are the nobler, more refined version of yourself. All educated men desire the best for others. You must seek the good of others by using the same controlled contemplation. Meditation requires you to imagine the other person as being or possessing the greatness that you want for him.Your desire to be with another person must be intense. You can rise above your current sphere through your desire. The road to fulfillment is

shorter if you imagine yourself as the embodiment of your desire for your friend or yourself. This is how I have learned to reach my greatest goals for others and myself. My own failures would prove me wrong if I said that I had mastered my attention control. However, I can say, along with an ancient teacher, "This one thing that I do is forgetting the things which are behind and reaching out unto those which are before." . For the prize, I press towards the mark."

286.   If two people agree... If two agree... A Law that can't be broken. You don't need to do anything outside. You can speak to yourself and then listen. The two could be in you. "State what you have in a bold and positive manner." . Which is what you really want. "I want it," you say. . It is not a hope. It is not a fact. We live in an imaginary world. This world is simply one's imagination "pushed out." The human imagination and God are one.

287.   Although you may not be able to see the effects of what your imagination has done, it is inevitable. There is no other creator who can stop it. Awareness is the key to all things. Without it, nothing is possible. The imagination claims that "I kill and make alive, I wound then I heal." I create the darkness and form the light. I create the darkness and make the good.

288.   All of the conflicts in the world are evidence that Imagination can and does run wild. Imagination is the only foundation. It is the Rock on which one builds his home. Whatever happens, don't blame anyone, but stay on that Rock. Christ (your wonderful Human Imagination), is He and the only cause of all the phenomena of existence. This truth will give you a solid foundation on which to build. You will find that this power is far more powerful than you could ever imagine. You will discover that you don't need anyone else's help. You only need to assume that you already have what you desire. Dare to make that assumption and walk towards it. Even if it takes a thousand people, they will all appear and perform their roles, without knowing why. They will do it without permission or consent, as they did with my friend's dream.

289.   It is possible to satisfy your desire through the act of imagination.

290.	It will be much easier to live if you believe you are the only one responsible for all of the events in your life. If life is too difficult to bear at times, you will find another cause. Man's inability to take responsibility for his own life creates Satans and devils. To see others other than yourself is to create a golden image. Asking for forgiveness from a priest. Despite being told not to call any man on Earth father, he calls him father. Man sees him as an authority and seeks to imitate a manmade image.

291.	Brook Atkinson's article is today in the New York Times. He just returned from Leningrad. When he began to return from Leningrad, they didn't bother to inspect his luggage concerning tobacco or liquor. This is what they all seek, as it generates revenue. They weren't concerned about ideas. They asked him: "Does he have any magazines?" He replied, "No." He also said, "No." This was the only question they had the second time. "Do you really mean that?" Are you carrying a Bible? They could also read. . They know both the Hebrew and the Greek languages. They could go back and discover the true meaning of God, which is "imagination". Hebrew "potter" means imagination. Who makes anything? Is it not possible that God created me from the clay and the dust? And I. . The made, and he . The maker. The creator was the imagination. After that, imagination submerged himself in the thing created and gave me myself.

292. If I could give the mood, the imagined mood or sensory vividness, it never failed me. It is easy to explain, and I could give you uncountable case histories.You know what you want and you can start to think about it. This is not enough. Now you must think FROM it. How could I think of it? I'm sitting here and want to be somewhere else. How can I imagine, as I sit here, being able to place my imagination in a space far removed from this room?

293.	So, "Be still, and know that God is in you." You don't have to be tied to what your senses say you are.

294.	We can control our inner dialogue and match it with our fulfilled wishes. Then we can put aside all other processes and act only by our imaginations.

295.   When we create the right sequence of events and then experience it in our imagination until it takes on the reality tone, we create conditions. This inner process is an activity that needs to be directed consciously. Through a series mental transformations we become more aware of the existing parts of what is. By matching our mental activity with that part of creation we want to experience, we activate, resurrect, and give life to it.

296.   It's easy. I am in touch with this state through my imagination. I visualize that I'm exactly where I want to be. How do I know if I'm there? One way to prove I am there is to describe what a man sees in his world. What the world looks like is entirely dependent on where I am standing when I observe it. If my world is described according to the point in space that I envision, then it must be true. I'm not physically there, no, but my imagination is. Wherever I am in my imagination, it becomes real. I will also go there in flesh. It is finished when I am in that state. It has never failed. This is how you can use your imagination to achieve your goals.

297.   Jesus Christ, your wonderful humanimagination and the eternal creative power God has given you, is what I am telling you. You don't know Jesus Christ if you don't know this! You might say, "He is a human being." But, you are one! Jesus Christ is God, the Father, and God the Spirit. Those who worship him believe in Sprit through their art of feeling. I have seen a state I imagined become a tangible fact I can share with others. This has been done many times, and I have also taught others how to do it. He is the only creative force in the universe, and I'm grateful that I found him.All that is happening in the world today can be shared with others because it was once imagined. You have discovered Jesus Christ, the creative power that brought all things into existence. Once you have found him, trust him and live by his principles. This will allow you to move into the stream of eternal living by fulfilling scriptures and knowing that "All power on earth and heaven is given unto my."

298.   We all think that a problem will solve itself. If we don't operate the problem, it will remain dormant. Imagination doesn't operate by itself.

299.   Imagine yourself in the fulfilled state you desire.300 This law states that all things are created from nothing, and that they must first be conceived before becoming conceived.

QUOTES 301 - 400

301.   The 12th chapter of Book of Numbers tells us: "If there's a prophet among you," but a scriptural prophet is one who listens to God and acts on it. If you asked me whether I was a prophet, I would say yes. I have fulfilled scripture, not by prophesying through a teacup leaf, cards, teacup leaves or astrology. I recognize that I am "the Father" in scripture. I came into this world to share my revelations and my experiences about the power to create. This is how God demonstrated his ability to create and his ability to recall when!You can feel wealthy even if you have nothing. I can recall when I was unknown. I can recall when I couldn't sell a book. I can recall the time I couldn't sell any of my books. I can recall ....Now, you fill in the events and fulfill your desires. I can recall when. These words don't imply memory. I hope that you will try to put yourself in an I

Remember to be in the moment and trust your memories. Memory is your amazing human imagination and the creative power of God's scriptures, Jesus Christ.

302.   Here is a very healthy and productive exercise for the imagination,something that you should do daily: Daily relive the day as you wish you had lived it, revising the scenes to make them conform to your ideals. Imagine, for example, that today's mail contained disappointing news. Rewrite the letter. Mentally revise the letter and adapt it to reflect the information you would like to have received. Let's say you didn't receive the letter you wanted. Imagine that you have received the letter.

303.   If you see the Lord as your wonderful human imagination and you desire something, you can simply imagine it. Then, you will be able to walk in that peace. You will find a peace like no other when you trust the Lord. You will never bow again before anyone or anything else. You will serve Him knowing that only your wonderful human imagination can be holy!

304.   Men go to church to pray to a god that doesn't exist. But God is the only one who makes man live. Without God, man would not be able to breathe. When you do find God, you should trust him implicitly. But I warn you, he will not take your orders! Only when you visualize your wish being fulfilled, will God act on it. As you lay down tonight, imagine the fulfillment of your wish in complete confidence. You should believe me so that you can also say, "I have believed in whom I have believed." When you find the Lord, your God, who is your amazing human imagination, you will never fail. He will teach you to trust him fully. You will learn to trust him completely, knowing that God does not need you to create the means to satisfy your desires.305. Through imagination, we can disarm and transform violence around the world.

306.   I believed Jesus Christ was my wonderful humanimagination. He was one with God and all things were possible for him. I knew that I couldn't force God to do anything. He would only do what I imagined!

307.   Believe in your human imagination, and you will be the rockupon for which he stands. He is your Lord and the only one you should serve. If you don't want to serve another person, you don't know God. If your boss says you should do the right thing and you get a raise, and you trust your boss, you don't trust God. You can't put your faith in anyone other than your amazing human imagination. God is the only creative power!

308.   Accept the fact that God is your wonderful humanimagination. Accept this idea and let it ferment. Accept your true self, and live with it. You might say, "It's easier for me to live with my husband (or wife) if it's not revealed." It was hard to do, but it caused chaos in our household. So we keep going to the same church and continue doing the same things in the outside

world. You must be open to admitting me to men. The Father who sees only the heart won't accept you if you are ashamed. Your beliefs from the past will be overthrown if you make any changes to your fundamental belief. Your belief that "I AM Rich" is true, but your world will change if you speak from the core of your new God concept. Do not be ashamed to admit to me what you have believed. Despite not having the experience to back your claims, you should not be ashamed to share the good news you have received from me.

309.   You may not realize it, but imagining something completely different about your life would change the way the world works. All imagination is in the world you create; the world doesn't know it.

310.   All phenomena of life are caused by the Human Imagination. "By him all things were created, and without him nothing was made that was made." Remember that your Human Imagination is the God of scriptures and the dreamer within you, so if anything or anyone happens to your world, it is your Human Imagination.

311.   If you are willing to accept the challenge, you can still exercise your power at this level. Take a look at yourself and ensure that you live up to the promise of your imagination! Do not let anyone else test you. Are you fully accepting the fact that Jesus Christ lives in you? If the answer is "not quite", then you have failed this test. You are a false Christ if you, like one million Christians, believe in another Jesus Christ. You will not find him in church or by giving to the poor. He is inside you, and only you can see it! No one can prophesy for your benefit! Only scripture is the only prophecy that you will fulfill.If someone tries telling me something about a medium or astrologer, I get annoyed so much that I want to shout "Have I ever heard you?" You worship false Christs if you believe all that nonsense! This principle will make you famous in this world. But I have a question for you: Are you in the mainstream of fulfillment scripture? Are you a true believer in Jesus Christ the Messiah, or are you merely imagining it? I'm here to tell you that there has never been another Christ, and that there will never be another Christ.

312.   You will be surprised to learn that Christ is in you the hope of glory. God's human imagination was made man so that man could become God. This mystery is one we are called to investigate, because the power that created the universe became you, so that you can be all-creative power as He is. This knowledge was not given to me by a man. It was not in my head.I have never heard of it from anyone else. It was shown to me that God is in man's amazing human imagination!

313.   This principle can be applied to all aspects of your life. This schoolroom is for you to use your imagination and have faith. You can imagine and create noble concepts for yourself and others, and you can live in them. In a way that you don't know, you will have an impact on the lives of all people in the world. Everyone who is needed to realize your dream will be attracted to it and brought to you. Even people who think they are cleverly stacking the deck against you will discover that they will be stacking the deck against themselves.When you imagine, everyone around the world is affected by your thoughts. It is possible to imagine what it would be like to be alone and not disturb the entire world. He is innocent and will not be charged. Although they can pinpoint the cause, they cannot fault him for being in a cell. He could still cause hatred from the depths of his own soul. It is important to think carefully. Only one being awakens, and that is God. We were placed in this schoolroom in love, even though we often cry, just like the children. These loving fathers sent their children to school, but they were not willing. A loving Heavenly father sent you here. It is your greatest talent, which you apply to the world. This is imagination.

314.   You have created a graven image if you consider a Jesus Christ other than your wonderful HumanImagination. When you find the true Christ,. . The Rock. . It is possible to build your house without any rumors or disagreements. If you build on the sand, your house will fall apart. But if your believe in your amazing Human Imagination, then you can create your own world. . Jesus Christ. . Nothing can destroy it. Your Imagination, Christ the

Christ, is dreaming inside you and creating your world. Give him noble thoughts. Be selective and try to do something for yourself.

315.   No matter what your dream may be, visualize it being fulfilled and trust God implicitly. It doesn't matter how many people are required to perform the role they need to in order to create what you believe you are. This is the world we live in. Jesus Christ is your amazing human imagination! Believe me.

316.   It takes some time to convince ourselves when reason and senses are not in agreement. If we were functioning at higher levels, all things would be subject to our imagination. It takes some time to reach this level. This is why it takes perseverance, patience, and diligence. These are the costs we have to pay in order to reap the rewards we seek. We must always remember the difference between a state and its occupant. A state is a permanent place that you are occupying. It could be poverty, wealth or health; it might be unknown in this world. . They are not states.You are not known or unknown. . You are immortal. You can assume you are and, to the extent that you believe you are, you will bear the fruits of that belief. . But you're neither poor nor rich. You are immortal and will inherit the entire universe. God created you as a unique individual, with God being the only one who can give it to you.

.

You and God are not the only ones who can see it. . only God, and you are him. This is the purpose.

317.   Tonight, test yourself! I won't test you. I'm not here to test anyone. I just urge you to look at yourself and see if your faith is being kept. Or are you going to call someone and tell them how terrible things are, and appeal to them on the outside? Do you believe in the power of God? Are you able to always look to your imagination? Do you keep faith in the state you have imagined? You have passed the test if you do. If every rumor or doubt can make you feel like a pawn on the chessboard of fear, you're not keeping the faith. You can decide what you want. Is it worth you trying to prove yourself? You can say, "I always go to my imagination whenever I   am faced

with a problem. And there is a solution." You have passed the test if you can do that. It's as easy as that.

318.   Believe me when i say that God is love. I was able to stand in his presence and he hugged me. Do you know that love is eternal death if it is separated from imagination? Let me tell you why. My friend is unemployed, without money, and overburdened beyond belief. He is someone I love, and I cannot deny that I love him. When I think about him, my memory reminds me of how poor he is. I will love him and keep him there until I learn how to use my imagination. The cup of experience is the only way to know imagination. We love our parents, mothers, wives, children and friends when we enter this world. But, we don't know how to transform them from the way they are. Unless we have the cup of experience and practice the great secret to imagining. This is why I believe that love without imagination is eternal death. God's greatest gift is imagination. He is love, yes. He has infinite wisdom and power, but his creative power lies in imagination.He gives you his creative power by giving you his Son Christ. This is the definition of Paul's second chapter to the Corinthians. As you continue to use your imagination about your friend, the world will mold him into the image of someone who is successful, happy, and debt-free. God's amazing gift to you makes all this possible.

319.   Let me tell you, we will remain in the world of death until our entry into themainstream and reach the climax. It is amazing to realize how this world is a world full of death. Your life is only as vivid as your imagination. Imagine everything as a symbol. Life is itself an activity. Your wife, your closest and dearest friend, as well as your father, mother, siblings, and brothers are all symbols. They all reveal who you are.

320.   It is not hard to see why he called himself the vine. He stated, "I AM THE VIENNA and YE ARE THE BrancheS." It is impossible for a branch to have life if it is not rooted in the vine. Every man on the planet is a branch. He is rooted in me, God, and ends in me. This can be said about every man on the planet. You can see me and hear me. Even though I just said, "You are rooted within me", you can also claim that I am rooted within you and that I end   in

God as much as you are rooted into and end in God. It is your responsibility to uplift every man in the world if you are aware of it. One must not be forgotten.Every person must be saved and your life is the way that this redemption happens. Discard no man. Each man can be changed. You can change any man by seeing him as he appears to be and asking him what he would rather be than what he is. Once you have a clear idea of what he wants to be, you can imagine him as that person. Talk to your loved ones and discuss this man as if it were a reality. If you can do this, you will see that the man you envision will be a reality.

321.	The beginning of all miracles is determined imagination.

322.	You are the Christ mentioned in scripture. Your own hope of glory is you. Jesus Christ is within you, and so can your human imagination. Why should anyone else need help? You are the one in whom imagination lives. You are the only Jesus Christ, I assure you.

323.	This is how water and spirit are born. You will believe me if I tell you that a false assumption can be made to become fact if it is persistently held. Water is not enough. It is important to grasp the spirit of it all and then apply that truth. If I can believe that I am the man that I want to become, and continue believing that, then I will gradually become that man. That knowledge is amazing. It is not possible to bring this being into existence by only using water. This is the one who was born by water and blood, according to our tradition. It wasn't water alone, it was water and blood. Also, while I do have the knowledge, I can't bring my ideal to life by just knowing it. It is up to me to put the knowledge into practice. When I do it, my savior is there and I am able to make him real by doing. This is how we celebrate Easter. This is your wonderful human imagination.

324.	Today, how many people can attribute their success or failure to their imagination? Average man will answer, "John Brown did it," or "The storm or the president." Only a few people will admit that their success or failure is due to their imagination. You are the only one who can create your life. Christ is in you. Your imagination can be used to make good or bad decisions. If you see God as a man of imagination you recognize the power behind the mask God is wearing. Instead of giving credit to the mask's wearer, praise Christ, the Christ-like one. Christ is the one who rises up from within us. Christ is the One who bears the name I AM. This is what Jesus, Joshua and Jehovah actually mean.325. This teaching (that Christ is our imagination), shocked and repulsed me at first . For I was a fervent and earnest Christian and didn't realize that Christianity couldn't be inherited from my parents by accident. It had to be consciously adopted as a way for life. . It stole my understanding later, through visions and mystical revelations, as well as practical experiences. I was able to interpret it in a deeper way. After drinking the water of psychological meaning, not one stone will remain of literal understanding.

326.   If Christ is the one who radiates from within you and byhim all things can be made, and without him not any made that is made (even bad), then you have to find him. Is it not Him who made your terrible day, your horrible month, and your awful year? You will be brutally honest with your self and admit that the events you experienced were related to your imagination. You will find him when you acknowledge and recognize this. Because He is a person and because you are a person, then you will know who He is. Keep your head high and know that you have learned from all your mistakes. Now you can start to envision the best you can be. You will then be able to awaken and join your brothers. "I AM NOT a God distant, in me lo I am one, forgiving every evil and seeking no acknowledgment." Why should I ask for recognition if we are one? Forgive all for they don't know what they do.

327.   You can now see your own inner vision and determine what you want in the world. You will see your Savior, Jesus, when you can identify what you want instead of what you have. Let Him go and let everything else go. You can let go of all the beliefs you once held and focus on the idea that YOU ARE the man you desire to be. This will take you to Calvary. Calvary is the ability to fix your mind on that state. This will bring you towards Easter, or that wonderful day we refer to as the Resurrection. You will make the state you have only ever imagined come alive. You will find fulfillment of the state if you are faithful to the concept. It is also known as rebirth in the Bible.

328.   Paul invites you in the 13th chapter 2 Corinthians to test God. Are you aware that Jesus Christ is within you? This is quite a challenge. If Jesus Christ is within you, and you believe he is your human imagination that creates reality, then you can put him to the test by imagining what you are. . At the moment,. . Your reason denies, and your senses deny. Can you believe in your imagination now? Is it possible to believe in your imagination, the true God? It's possible. Imagine yourself as the person you want to be. Consider how it would make you feel if this were true. Because feeling creates life. This principle is outlined in Scripture.According to Isaac, Isaac was blind at the time he said, "Come near, my son. That I may feel you." He couldn't see what he was presuming so he sought out the feeling. The scriptures contain the blind father calling out to his son to feel and be touched. Joseph, who admitted to being blind, placed his sons in front of Jacob. He crossed his arms as he blessed them. This justified his actions. Let me ask you, what would it feel like to have your desires fulfilled? What would it feel like to be the man you desire? Believe in Jesus Christ and feel the sensation. It is possible to visualize everything, but faith is required to make it real. As I stated earlier, first you have to hear it. Then faith will bring acceptance.

329.   Jesus Christ, your I AM is the Word sent to transform you. You are the creator of everything. Even though you may seem limited and incapable of creating anything, you can still see it all in your imagination. If you can imagine a state and remain faithful to it, it will come alive for your. If I am made everything, and you know that you imagined it before it came to pass, then Jesus Christ is your wonderful human imagination.

330.   "He was in all the world, and all the world was made by him. The world knew him not." Did you know that imagination created the entire world? You may not realize that imagination can change the world. You might be surprised to know that your world will change if you start to think differently about your life than what the wise say. All imagination is in the world you create; the world doesn't know it.

331.   So, I warn you about the law and let you make your own decision. I have no control over this. It is impossible to stop. You can't have me acting

like a mother and telling you that you shouldn't do this. According to the Book of Deuteronomy, "I place before your this day good or evil, life or death, blessings and cursing; choose Life." He says that you should choose life, but he cannot take away the right, which he has given you, to choose whatever you like. He will do what you want, even if it is not the best for you. It will also boomerang, but it will happen. Because you can imagine any thing in this world, imagination creates reality. The man who imagined it. . If he can imagine it and continues to believe in it, it will happen. That's the law.

332.   The "Wisdom in this world is foolishness to God" is what he has learned. He is rising to a world where his imagination will rule. All things in the world will fall under his control. God, who has given himself to man, God is all-wise and he will be all-wise. God, being all-powerful and all-loving will be all-powerful and all-loving because he gives himself to mankind. You will never be replaced and everyone will be equal before God because God is God. He cannot give you more than he has given you. One cannot be more than the other, because God gave you yourself, as if there were only God and you. Only you.

333.   He is the world, the world made him. Yet, the world does not knowhim. Walking along the streets, man imagines the world around him, but he cannot recognize his own harvest.

334.   "Born not by blood, of the will or flesh of man or of the will or flesh of the flesh, but of God." This is a completely different birth. It will occur in the person who discovers Imagination, trusts him implicitly, believes in him and holds on to him. You must first alter your imaginal structure to prove that imagination can cause change. Once your world is a picture of your thoughts, then you will have found him. You will then realize the truth of the 14th verse. The Word will be found in you. The Word has become flesh and is now dwelling within you, full of grace & truth. Jesus Christ is more than a historical figure. Jesus Christ became flesh and lives in us.

335.   You cannot imagine anything other than what is. Eternityexists. You can imagine what you want to become. You can also slip into the past to live the event you want. We dream the life we want until we wake up.

Therefore, I advise you to pray for God. . Your own amazing human imagination. . You are the source of your dreams.

336.   You would be amazed at how deep your inner self (which is your human imagination) is trying instruct you. It takes God a while to reach your surface mind from the center. While he's moving, He is also influencing your surface mind. When He arrives, you and Him will no longer be two. It is easy to tell when He is approaching the surface. He starts questioning the reality of the world in his life.

337.   Christ is your imagination. Christ is power and wisdom of God. This power and wisdom creates all things in the world. It is possible to trace an imaginal act from my own existence that was made into a fact. Then I repeated it until it became a fact. It is possible to repeat the imaginal act and make it more concrete. I have found that power within myself. The Bible refers to him as Christ and describes his presence as a man. . But that man is Jesus. Jesus Christ is the resurrected power that has been resurrected, and this is why he is called the "God now." He is now called "the Lord" and all should bow before him when it happens. You will be amazed when you have that experience.You won't believe anyone; no one is going to believe that you are more than the first person to whom it happened. But he is the one who rose from the dead and no one believed him. Who would believe this story up to the end? They wanted a different Messiah. A conquering hero who would appear just like a man from a glorious background of soldiers and conquer the enemy of Israel. This would bring Israel victory. They are always looking for this kind of Messiah. They are everywhere today, the false Messiah's that promise to lead the nations to victory, even temporary. This is not Messiah. Messiah doesn't have anything to do with this world. He is resurrected from this world. This world is disappearing, just like a fading.

garment. Christ in man is power and wisdom. Then, the inman that is man's imagination becomes a mercy, because he uses it lovingly.

338.   Scripture encourages you to evaluate yourself, to see if Jesus Christ is in you. If all things are made by him, and without him there is no thing made that is made. Who is he? I will tell you who he really is. He is your wonderful human imagination. How can I be sure that this is true? Imagine a state and then be faithful to it. Then watch it happen in my world. My belief in God made all things possible, and I can trace the origin of my desire state back to my imagination.

339.   Tell me, the God you once believed in was God is now your own wonderful human imagination. You can put him to the test. Create a scene that reflects your fulfillment of desire. . To the best of your abilities . It will merge with you. Do you realize that if you are able to move into the scene, it will be objective before it is seen? It will be as objective as the world. When you break the spell, what was only objectively real a moment ago will now be to you as a dream. But you will know that it is. You can then wait with confidence for it to happen, and share it with others. They may believe it or not, but you should tell them that we are all one. This is the eternal story.

340.   This is a vivid example of a duplicate dream. Scripture tells us that if the dream is repeated, it is fixed. The Lord will soon bring it to pass. My friend is witness to God's creative power. He now knows that God is his amazing human imagination. The great I AMness of man is God, and all things are possible for Him. The challenge now is on him. He can have whatever he wants! He just needs to adjust his thinking to what he wants until the state becomes alive in him. The state will then become his world.

341.   A lady who can go back and merge with the past can recall an experience from long ago. A man can also travel into the future to interview the people that will be taped on Friday. . Where is the experience from the past? And where is Friday's show next Friday? Are we just focusing on certain states, or is everything already complete? This is a dream that you can alter or completely change. You are often called upon to change or even eliminate something in your daily life. This is your human imagination.

342.   However, you can still use his name through Moses until that is revealed. "And tell them when you speak to them that 'I AM' sent me unto them." Let them go out of the wilderness and into the light by my name. No

matter where you might be, regardless of whether you feel lost or unwanted, unemployed, or even if you believe you are, you can take charge of your life today. . You can transform these barren states into states of fruition. Simply imagine "I AM" and then you can hear, smell, and see the world around you. If you stay true to what you're hearing and imagining, it will be externalized in your world. It's not worth judging before you actually try it.

343.   Do not forget the law of God, which is: An assumption can become a fact. Fiction is impossible if an assumption creates its reality. While I might forget what I assumed today, and I may not recognize the harvest that I have harvested, it would not have entered my world if I hadn't brought it in through an imaginal act.344. We have the power to imagine anything we

want to

be.

345.   You can imagine everything as you want them to be, regardless of your senses denial or reason. Once you do that, you will feel the joy of accomplishment and you will rest in confidence that you have achieved your goal. . Then you will be the one they refer to in scripture. Did you know that all things were made by him, and that without him nothing was ever made?

346.   You are the creator of your amazing human imagination, Jesus Christ. There has never been another. You will experience Him one day, and you will feel the love of his life. You will forget everything you did as a man in this mortal world. This is why you must go through all the mess and mire of this world in order to see this seed emerge. When it does, you become one with God, who alone is perfect, and all of your past is erased as if it never was.

347.   Imagination is the source of all that exists in your world. It is impossible to imagine anything that wasn't first imagined. However, when you see it objectively, you lose sight of its origin and don't realize that it was created by you. Everything that appears without is first an image. It was only a dream created by you, the Lord Jesus Christ.

348.   Do not forget the principle of your amazing imagination. Itlovingly advocate for everything. You are pushing out the world. Imagine it and then let go.

349.   You can only imagine the God you worship. You will discover that he is the one who creates everything by proving his reality through what you did. No one can convince you that this was an accident.

350.   Concerning the Law, I am unable to provide any information beyond a basic understanding of the Law. You will have to make your own decision and take the risk. However, we do have scripture for the Law. . It doesn't matter what their Law knowledge is. The 18th chapter of Matthew contains these words: "If any of you on earth agree about any request you must make, my Heavenly Father will grant that request." If you find two, then that request will also be granted. Can you imagine something more? If two people agree to any request, . It doesn't need to be perfect, it doesn't have to look like this or that, but it can be any request. . "That you must do, that request will also be granted by my Heavenly father." This is the greatest secret about the human imagination. We are told that "With God, everything is possible." Next, he says: "All things can be done by him who believes." He then equates God and the human imagination, stating that God is the human imagination and that all things are possible for the human imagination.

351.   God, in your imagination, cannot be farther away than to be close, for the nearness implies separation. I am everywhere you are! To claim that God is another is to say "I AM" near. . There is none other. God and you are one because He is your amazing human imagination!

352.   God can dream in you, and you can test him at any time if your alert. He steals from your conscious mind most disguised as creative fancy. Imagine a friend, and sit down to watch the amazing, moving being create mental images. Your amazing human imagination is the God of the Universe. He is in your depth and underlying all your faculties, including perception. You suddenly find him moving in a serpentine fashion in the form creative fancy. You can think of anyone you like and you'll be able to catch Him.

353.   If you make a change in the outside world and I am aware of it, then the same change will occur within me. It could be socially, intellectually or physically. But if I am exposed to the change, it will penetrate me. Acceptance of the change will allow me to alter my perception of you. Do I have to wait for the change to manifest on the outside in order to change my perception of you? Or can I first create the change inside and then observe the outside change. If I realize that the potter is part of my amazing human imagination, I can do it. "O Lord, thou art my Father, we are the clay. Thou art our potter; we are the works thy hand." The Lord, the potter, and the Father are one being. They share the same awareness. The same imagination. Trust me! Believe in your imagination! All things are now possible because God has reproduced himself within you. You must first create changes inside if you want to see them. Permeate what is within you. That penetration will cause the outside to follow the path you have taken. You can only prove it by trying it. Imagine the scene that would occur after you have achieved your dream.

354.   Everybody in the world is producing fruit. . Being known, being unknow, and everything in between: poverty, wealth, health. . You know the law and can take anyone from the place you found them to the one you want. His consent and knowledge are not required. Tell him not to tell anyone. This power is within you. You can convince yourself that the imaginal act you're describing is true and real. Once that happens, it becomes real. So I say to you, if anyone forgives you, he is forgiven. If you keep his sin, it is retained. If he doesn't find the job he wants, don't be hard on him. You won't argue with him. Do you think he needs a job? If so, tell him to get a better job and to put in more effort. This principle is not being applied. You can only forgive him if you are convinced that he is working. Sin is missing the mark. You can help him if he fails to see it. Listen to these words: "If they had not come and spoken unto us, they would not have known sin." He shows men that causation can be mental and not physical. . And now, man doesn't have any excuse for his sin of missing the mark.

Man has an imagination if he has a brain. He can use it. He says, "You've heard that adultery is forbidden. But I tell you, if you look at a woman lustfully, you have already committed the act in you heart." He holds every man accountable for failing to achieve the goal. He doesn't condemn me if I don't get the job. He asks me to follow the law as it is written. "They clearly read the law of God from the book, and they gave the meaning so that people understood it." He reads from God's Word (God's revealed Word), that causation can only be mental, and that imaginal actions create facts. What are you imagining then?

I can tell you that I have the thought for you every day, morning, noon and night. I hope you understand it. I have to convince myself that there is nothing else in this world. This is what he told us to do. You will see the day come, it happens in a moment you least expect. Then suddenly everything awakens and the flower starts to bloom in you.

355.   It is very different to be awake and asleep to your imaginations. You can see the cause of an event happening on the outside when you are awake. But if you're asleep, you will be able to find the cause. Causation, however, is only within the person who observes the effect. Causation is represented by the foot in both the 40th and the 69th Psalms as well as the 10th chapter in Romans. All things will be under his feet in the end.

356.   My belief is that imagination creates reality. If this is true, then your life will be filled with the results of your imagination. Even though I have altered the words, I believe what I am saying remains unchanged. Scripture says that you can believe you will receive whatever you want. This principle is a two-hundred-year-old one, but Jeremiah also tells the story of the potter with his clay. But imagination is not a normal part of your natural currency of thought. You will not be able to act conscious until it becomes part of you. This awareness, like breathing, must become so integral to your being that it is not possible to blame or praise anyone. It doesn't matter if your life started behind an eight-ball or in a palace. You will soon realize that you are   always

externalizing the world you imagine. You can't reproduce your environment if you don't know this principle. . It can be pleasant or it can be unbearable . As long as your imagination is fed by your senses, you can continue to imagine the future for ever. This principle allows you to ignore the present and allow you to imagine it as you want it to be.357. Man lives by being committed to invisible states. He fuses his imagination with other things, and experiences the effects of this union.

358.   I now know that Man is all Imagination and God is Man. He exists in us and we are him. The Eternal Body is Man's Imagination. Jesus is His divine body, and we are His members. This is because He can make all things, and I can imagine it. He is not someone I am separated from, but my wonderful human imagination.

359.   As in the past, today's men can't believe that imagination is responsible for the phenomena of modern life. While they can envision a beautiful picture on canvas and have it printed, they will not be able to relate that same process to a toothache. But there is only one cause. Only one cause exists: I, the Lord, am it. There is no God except me. I create light and make darkness. I create weal and woe. I am the Lord. He does all of these things. Your misfortune is not your fault. Although you could argue that a friend betrayed you trust and caused your troubles, it is not true. Your dream inspired your friend to help you. Causation does not come from the outside. You will discover that there is only one God. He is your amazing human imagination.

360.   Every scriptural miracle can be described as an acted parable. The journey of life begins when imagination enters the boat called man. Then, the financial, marital and physical storms that follow are based on man's dreams. He can dream of something beautiful and experience happy, healthy storms. He will not be able to see that his imaginal activity is the cause of his weal until the disciples awaken him. You are now aware of all the thoughts that you create every minute of your life. This awareness can be carried into your dream world. For. . Knowing the cause and the world you want to create. . You will always be aware of what you're imagining. You won't be able to seek

out your desires in the world, but you will look within and find them all waiting for fulfillment in God's temple.

361.   Words are essential to thinking. You may find someone you like looks amazing when you meet him. This is just a thought. It's not spoken in audible words. You can be sure he is well, and that you sent your message. Consider the positive news that you just heard about your friend. He is so rich that he doesn't know what to do. Although you may be able to hear his laughter, feel the reality of what you are saying and allow it to happen. Do not try to predict how it will happen, just accept it as a physical reality. That is how you can know the power and influence of your words. God became flesh and blood and man was made to be God.You may wonder why there is a disturbance in the world, but you can't control your imagination. While it may be fun to argue with your family, friends, parents, or other people from ridiculous premises, if you realize that all things must come about, then why are you doing this? You can believe that every thought is responsible for what it implies. If so, stop having negative or undesirable thoughts and start a new one. One day, this fundamental revelation about the unfolding of God's word will come to pass. The sacred word of God will be revealed and you will play the central role. You will then discover who Jesus is.

362. Imagination is the only faculty of the mind that can create objective conditions.

363.   He will not have the same sense of Christ in his imagination until he has the ability to see all things objectively without subjective relationships.

364.   Do not believe people who claim Jesus Christ is returning. Jesus Christ has never left your side. He did not say, "Lo,I AM with you always," so how are you supposed to expect him to return? Scripture says that Christ was raised into the kingdom of Heaven (which is inside) and that he will return in the same way as he was lifted up. Christ (God's creative power) cannot come

from outside if Christ is within you. Christ is not visible, but he has never left you.

365.   Today's newspaper contained an article stating that scientists have discovered that the so-called "throne Peter" was only 900 years old. The chair has been removed from its protective cover and is being kept as a holy relic. It was once a piece wood on which some self-proclaimed nut sat, while claiming to be the emperor or pope. After a thousand years of absurdity, the truth is now known.What is man to do if he doesn't want to believe that he is in control of his own destiny and that God is only his imagination? You may believe you have nothing to do with the creation of the world, but in reality you had. Its purpose is not yet known to you, so you don't know what it is. You were able to limit and limit your creative power and make your world even more expansive. God is always expanding his illumination. He took on himself the limit to contraction, the limit to opacity, called man, so that he could break the limitation and grow. It's all the glory.

366.   The "I remember when" principle is both destructive and constructive. As you see rubble, you can say "I remember when this building was magnificent" and then look at it again. You can also stand on rubble and tell yourself: "I remember when it was all rubble," to evoke a magnificent building. Or you can say, "I recall when my friend had nothing" or "I recall when he was so rich," to indicate that he is now sick. You can see the power in that revelation. You can use your imagination however you wish, but you are responsible for the operation of your creative powers. You decide and you are responsible for the impact it has on the world.

367.   Never let anyone tell your that Jesus is coming back. He has never left you. Christ is crucified within you, in your wonderful human imagination. He will soon awaken in all of us as he gathers together into himself, into one body, one spirit, one God, and Father of all.

368.   Take a look at yourself in the mirror. See radiant health and happiness reflecting back to you. You will be able to regain your former self-image if you keep looking in the mirror. Your image, or your idea of yourself,

is in your wonderful human imagination, who is Christ, and Christ is the only God. God the Father and Christ, your creative power, are one entity. He has never left you!

369.   Now, imagine your friend is well. Imagine your daughter married. Remember when you were single as you go through your life. Have you ever heard someone say, "Who is he?" You may have heard them say, "I remember when he had everything and was a nobody!" This is because envy adds fuel to the statement and causes the other to have more. Although he may not know the exact cause of his success, he can remember that it was an act of intense remembrance.

370.   You can now begin to transform every living thing in your world into love. But love without imagination is eternal death. You don't know if you are dealing with a situation. You can love someone deeply but keep him in an unlovely condition forever. You can free him by using your imagination. This world of experience is for a divine purpose. To know imagination. You can overcome the last enemy in the world, but the world is already dead. . The enemy of death . Imagine your friend as noble, desired, and loved. Then watch him transform into it. You can save your friend from poverty by saving yourself!It will happen. Don't worry about when or how it will happen. The world is yours, and everything within it. To be made alive, you must be separated from the Father and drop into the ground. A seed that falls into the ground dies, but it can remain alone if it does. Your imagination, the creative power of your mind, is what makes you a seed (the red earth that we call Adam). Your seed awakens when you hear the truth and apply it to your life.

371.   You are aware of your dreams tonight, no matter how beautiful or terrible they may be, because Christ has never abandoned you. Your imagination (Christ) is with you when you wake up in the morning. Without it, you would not be able to remember your dreams. Because imagination is the creative power that makes the world go round, the human imagination is the God they honor. You will soon discover how to harness your imagination and push the world out of you.

372.   All I have to do to help you or anyone else is to imagine I have heard them. Then I can hear what they tell me. There are then two: the one I hear and me, who is listening and hearing. Two people can agree to testify. Because imagining creates reality it must be externalized in my world. "The entire vast universe is just the imaginal act of "pushed out". And so we are told: "With God all things are possible" and "All things can be done by him who believes." Am I not equating God to the believing one? The believing one is not one's human imagination. It's that simple.

373.   As we can see objects in space, imagination is not possible. However, it can be seen that imagination cannot be observed. Fawcett gave the name "God", to the cause of all things, and said: "God, creator, is like pure imagination in ourselves." He is in our souls, beneath all our faculties including perception. His thoughts flow into our surface minds least disguised as productive fancy. You will hear God's voice if you listen to your thoughts. Unfelt thoughts produce nothing. A thought that produces motor elements reproduces itself. You will be able to see God in anger, fear, frustration, or congratulating you. Then you will know what's going to happen in your life. Unless you stop thinking and revise your thoughts. Most people are unaware of what they are doing and don't observe their creator.We can still catch him when he flows into our surface minds least disguised as productive fancy. You can make a difference in your life by reacting to a comment while you are riding the bus, driving the vehicle, at home, at work, or at the bar. If you're willing to accept its responsibility, this principle will set you free. Regardless of whether you accept it or not, your motor elements will be fulfilled regardless. You will not condemn or sympathize with anyone, but you can simply tell them about the principle. . If they agree to it. . Let the principle be a guideline in their lives.

374.   Your own amazing human imagination is the only cause of all the miracles of life. There is no other power. This is the God mentioned in Scripture. This is the only God. . Your own amazing human imagination. Are you able to envision what you would like tonight? It's okay. Don't minimize it. It doesn't matter what size it is; just state it and then listen with your wonderful voice to the matter. You can also tell a friend, without him

knowing. A friend may tell you that they heard good things about you. You already know what you want. It is possible to write it down in your head and then share it with a friend who knows you well. . Listen to his voice, he's confirming it. These are the ones who agree. In the sense that you allow him into your world, you don't need to hear another person's voice.

375.   According to Job, when he forgot himself and prayed for his friends, his captivity was lifted. All that Job had seemed to have lost was returned, and multiplied one hundred times. You can forgive someone by thinking about him as you want him to be, and then persuading your self of the reality of what you imaginal act is. This will allow you to forgive him for the things he does not deserve. You are substituting a noble idea for an ineffable one. That's forgiveness! This is forgiveness. It tests one's ability and willingness to accept the opposite nature. A priest might say, "I forgive you", but he will still remember what he said when he sees you walking down the street. He has not forgiven if he cannot remember! To erase the memory of what was said or done, something must be substituted.

376.   I want you to consider me serious. Your imagination will take you to where you want it to be. Imagine a scene that would make you feel like you have it. Be convinced of the truth of it and continue to believe in it. It is true. It is possible to believe it is true, and it will happen. If you believe it is true, imagination will not fail.377. To the imaginative man, everything is a manifestation the mental activity that goes on in man's mind without the senseuous reasonable man being conscious of it.

378. Imagination is the first step in the formation of all forms. Faith is the substance from which they are made. The imagination awakens the unconscious or latency of what is already there and gives it form.

379.   All of us are one. If I can stand right now and let my imagination take over, I will have an impact on the whole world. . Influencing anyone who can help me to objectify what I am imagining. Do it with love. Whatever you

do, do lovingly, . . It doesn't matter what it is. If you're ever in doubt, do what is right. This simple rule, known as the "Golden Rule", can be used to guide you. You can't go wrong with the rule of "Do unto other as you would like them to do unto you".

380.   Let me tell you, you can do anything you want! You can let people be who they want to be and set goals for your future. The power of the universe is within you, no matter what you have experienced in your life. The Lord Christ Jesus, whose Name is I AM, is that power. It is only after you put him to the test that you will discover Jesus Christ is within you. Christ was somewhere outside of space, I was taught. But, I accepted the challenge and tried it out for myself to find that I am creative.I believe that I create my life from within, and that it is my fulfillment of my own imagination. My choices have not always been wise. I've imagined things that were unlovely and then reaped the rewards by being the fulfillment of my imagination. After becoming more aware, I realized I could see Christ in my thoughts even though he was not disguised as a creative thought. If my thoughts were motor driven, and they were unpleasing, I would know what to expect unless it was revised. However, they were either pleasant or not so I knew that I would meet them.

381.   I must believe in John if I understand John correctly. Who is this being? My imagination. If IDo not believe it, but test it. . Even though I fail, . Well then, I don't believe in Christ. Christ is actually my imagination, your imagination. You can imagine a beautiful thing about another person, but if you don't believe that reality, you don't believe Christ. You can attend church every day, and donate ten percent of your income to your church choice. . All of these things are wonderful, so feel free to give them a try if you feel the same way. . But that is not Christ. This is not faith in Christ. Believe in Christ means to see another person in the world and feel a warm feeling towards him. Now, imagine him as if it were true and believe in the reality that you have done mentally.

All things are possible for Christ if you believe in him. Take him in front of your mind's eyes and let him see you as he wants to be seen. You do it, and you believe in the reality. This is faith in Christ. It is amazing how it works. It is because "All things are by a law Divine in each other's being."

You can reshuffle all the cards at the moment you are causing interference in his life. Everything will then be mirrored to reflect the change in him. Everyone in the world that can help bring about that change without their consent or knowledge. It doesn't matter if you need their consent. If they are able to be used to externalize your thoughts, they will. God will resurrect you even when you least expect it. You will then live it, and you'll be stunned at what God did for your life.

382.   He now asks me and all those who have read his letter to put ourselves to the test: "Testyourself. Do you not realize that Jesus Christ lives in you?" And he did all of these things. . Let's put him to the test. He is our imagination. That is the power, the creative power in the universe. Take a look around. Is there anything that you don't know about the world man created? . From the clothes he wears to his homes . That wasn't the first thought. Is there anything in the world that can be now proven as fact? . It was only imagined and then externalized. Yes, it was done with hands and the tools of the world. But, it all began as an image. An image is the result of man's reforming imagination-making faculties. If "All things were made through him" and "without him was not any made that was made," then I cannot draw other conclusions than that Christ of scripture was my imagination.

383.   I ask that you take the same responsibility. You must not give the blame to anyone, any organization, situation or circumstance. Instead, you should discover that imagination can create reality. If God is the cause of all existence, then God must also be your imagination. Because you can imagine, then . Like God . You are your own pure imagination. You can believe anything, regardless of what your senses say.

384.   If you allow it, the divine gift of reason will be taken from you and you will become poor. You have the ability to imagine anything you want, provided you remain faithful to what you've assumed!

385.   Everything in the world is God's creation. God is allImagination. Even the clothes and chairs we use are originally imagined, then made into existence. This is not a lie. People who say you should kill your desire are not going far enough. If I wanted to kill my desire, I would need to begin with the desire to not desire. And where would I go? What is the limit? Go out there and achieve your goals. This is what someone without an academic background will tell you. I'm going to go out on a limb and tell you that the Bible is true at a higher level. However, it is revealed metaphorically because man has confused literal truth with metaphor. I don't crawl on my stomach and no little serpent spoke directly to me, but what it means is true in metaphor.The serpent is the most subtle creature of all. It represents wisdom, which takes all his religions and arts for himself and dedicates them all to the creator. Then comes Blake, who shows them the reality of life. Now, those who believed themselves to be so smart are literally crawling on their stomachs in the presence such as he. The Bible is a book that tells things on a higher level. I have mystical experiences and I know things that I couldn't find in any other book.

386.   Creator of the world is in your deepest soul. He flows into your surface mind most disguised as creative fancy, but it can be seen in all of your faculties including perception. You will see Him creating in your thoughts. He is your very self! You are creating your world every moment. If you don't forget what you are seeing and it comes to fruition, you've found the creator. God is pure imagination, the only creator. If you can imagine a state, and it comes to pass, then you have found Him. Remember that God is your consciousness, your I AM, so whatever you imagine, God is actually creating it. You may not be able to recognize your harvest if you forget what you imagined. You may not recognize your harvest, regardless of whether it is good or bad. But if you forget how it came to be, you aren't finding God.

387.   Let me now tell you a story that I am familiar with, the story about my father. His father was a poor white man who was born on the Island of Barbados. My mother was poor. He had everything, she had nothing. They had children. Twelve children were born; two died at birth, ten survived. He didn't have anything. I don't know how he did it, but he was listening to me speak in New York City for the first time on Sunday morning. When we returned to our apartment, he said that everything he had said about his morning was true. Why do you tell people to shut their eyes? Keep your eyes open. Keep your eyes partially closed.Your imagination can be controlled and your attention can be managed if your eyes aren't closed completely. You might believe that I am simply sleeping off, if you see me sitting in my chair in the morning after breakfast. I'm not sleeping off anything. Then, I'm doing my day's job. I can bring to my mind the men I wish to work with on that particular day and I am in control of the conversation. As if it were true, I tell them exactly the things I want. They told me. . It is true. Then, when I feel satisfied with my inner conversation I go to town. It works this way.

388.   Jesus did not violate the law of Caesar. He looked at a coin and said, "Render unto Caesar all that is Caesar's." Ask your heavenly Father for more taxes if Caesar asks. If you imagine you have the money, you can ask him to give it to Caesar.

389.   While we're here, let's learn the rules of life and play it. The assemblage of mental states is what creates life. Mentally, my friend heard the words he would hear in his heart if his wish for his friend was fulfilled. The event was created by his mental assemblage. Once you've assembled your mental state, and allowed it to happen within you; you don't have to do it again. The moment you feel relief, you can throw your bread on the water. Relief is possible, even if you don't feel a physical sensation in a sexual way.You wait anxiously for the key to unlock the door when someone you love is sick. When they speak, you feel a sense of relief. This is exactly the kind of relief that you'll feel if you can imagine correctly. You are not supposed to repeat the same act every day. Although you can imagine the act over and over, you will only impregnate once. If you reach relief, your bread is cast upon the water to return in a matter of minutes. I have heard the phone ring.

. It was only minutes later that I had imagined it. . It is important to confirm that it happened. Sometimes it takes days, weeks or months. I don't repeat the action after I feel the relief and I know that there is nothing else I need.

You are subconsciously playing this game every day. Learn how to be conscious about it. Millions of people who receive relief believe the government owes their living. But there is no government. Only we pay taxes. The government doesn't have any money and can only provide what they need from our pockets. People on relief complain that they don't get enough money. This mood continues throughout the day. They don't see any change in their mood and can recognize no connection between what they like and what they don't like. They would not believe that their mood is responsible for the events in their lives. Although it is not what anyone wants, the truth is that there is no other cause. God is the only cause, and man is his own amazing human imagination.

390.   You may not believe it, but I have seen Godand you as one great Imagination. There is no other God. One day, the Imagination within you will awaken. . Fully aware of who and what you are. . You will realize that all things are yours. This is your destiny.

391.   You can imagine your reality, I promise you! You must be aware of what ideas others are forming in your mind if you want to make a difference in your life. If you encounter someone negative, try to put a positive idea in his place. Imagine him telling you something sweet every time you think about him. You now live in a world where he isn't disturbed by negative thoughts. He will not know that you are the source of his negativity because he won't be able to think negative thoughts anymore. It will be obvious to you and that is what is most important. You will live a happier life if you become more aware of your thoughts. It doesn't matter what other people do, if you can plant loving, kind thoughts, you will be blessed.

392.   You should shape your world from within, not from without. Be the person you want to be perceived by others. Assume they are true. . Because God is unstoppable. . You will see and experience what He has in mind. Because I AM, you are one with God. Our God, the Lord, is one I AM and not two! Define what you want to be, if God's IAM and yours is the same IAM. Believe that you are the Lord. Like the woman who turned a streetcar into an automobile. Your world outside will remain the same, but you can let yourself be lost in the new state.

393.   Feeling is essential for creativity. It is perfectly normal to want to transcend the present. If man were not unhappy with himself, there would be no progress in the world. We naturally want to live a happier life. It is normal for us all to desire greater understanding, better health, and greater security. In the 16th chapter of the Gospel of St. John it is stated that "Heretofore ye have not asked for anything in my name; request and ye will receive, so your joy may be complete."Humanity needs a spiritual revival. But by spiritual revival, I mean a genuine religious attitude in which each person accepts the challenge to embody a higher value of themselves, as Dr. Millikan did. The wisdom of a nation is not greater than the wisdom it produces in its units. This is why I believe in self-help. If we are passionate about this type of self-help (that is, if it embodies a higher and more complete version of ourselves), then all other types of assistance will be available to us. The ideal we strive to attain is available for a new form, but it cannot be born unless it is given human parentage. It is important to affirm that we already are the person we want to be, and to live like that, knowing, as Dr. Millikan, this assumption, although false to the outside world, will become a fact if we persist in it.

394.   Let's get back to the theme of tonight: Imagining creates Reality! What if you have imagined something but it didn't happen? What are you thinking right now? Do you think you're John Brown? John Brown was not something you knew when you were born. Others began to call your name John after you were born. As you grew older, you assumed you were John Brown. You began to respond to the name John when you heard it. Did you ever forget how secure you felt when you imagined it? Do you think you feel secure right now?Although you may not have any evidence of your security, you can allow

others to tell it to you. Your imagination will make it a reality. You already have the reality!

395.   Everyone will receive it because everyone will be resurrected. These bodies are wonderful for us and are filled with all the passions. . But it's not the body you will be wearing. You won't be able to control the organization of your sex. This type of creativity is unnecessary. Your imagination will awaken completely and you can create as much as you like. This is what we call reality, this amazing world that we live in today. . Let me tell you, I've seen it. . It is all imagination.These garments will be made after man has fulfilled his role and God has accomplished his purpose (which was to bring forth from him and make us all gods with Him). . It is made up all elements that feel permanent and wonderful. . They will disappear like smoke. There isn't an element that was not created by God's creative power, his amazing divine imagining. It is sustained in me because God sustains it through his imaginal act. All the elements will melt when he stops his imaginal act, and all will vanish. However, you and I will be lifted above all of it into an entirely new world, an everlasting world.

396.   He is an imaginative man, but he doesn't realize that everything he encounters is part of him.

397.   You are blessed when you can imagine for another, because there is no other. Listen to your friend's good news and feel the joy. Then let it happen in your world. Recognize your harvest. Recognize that you are responsible for its consumption. You are the only one who can make the world go around. Ask yourself what you want, and then go for it! It will happen. Don't be afraid to ask how.

398.   God is divine imagination. He limits himself to human imagination's limit and dies. The cry of the cross is true. He suffered complete amnesia as he gave himself completely to us. This was divine imagining being human imagining.We then build our little world. . It is beautiful, as it is for many of us. . It is so different and the power that we exert is so fragile, in comparison with the same power when raised and when the great name,

which is above all, is conferred upon you. You will be able to bear the name Jesus without losing your identity. . That power is a result of the name having infinite power. . Without losing your identity. All will be known and glorified together. The gift is unlimited. It is possible to use it more than others but the gift, Christ Jesus' gift, will remain the same.

399.	You will find the only God behind the mask that you wear. The DivineImagination reproduced itself in you as your human imagination. Because Divine Imagination includes all, all is contained within the human imagination. You will one day realize this and realize that the world is your creation, just like God created it. This knowledge will awaken in you and you will find that your Divine Imagination begins to expand for you. . Human imagination and God's Divine Imagination . One creator.

400.	From personal experience, I know that Jesus Christ is your amazinghuman imagination. The human imagination is buried in you and unfolds in you as scripture fulfills itself. You are the human imagination. Without realizing it, you can imagine everything and create all the miracles of life. You are unable to use your imagination. . as the enemy of Christ . Refrain from what I'm telling you. You'd rather go to Mass and light your candle than stay in church. People have written me letters claiming that I am a devil. However, I know they will one day wake up and all their past actions will be forgotten. These are the things they do and say because they are trying to find their inner strength.They are the sinners who cannot believe their amazing human imagination is God. . Judas, a sinner, betrays Christ. Tell the sinners in the world that they are the cause of all the phenomena of life. They will be furious and resentful. They don't believe that God, the only God, loved us enough to give His life for us so that we might be as He is. They will attempt to discredit the revealer, refusing to accept the truth. He was instructed to "Lead Him Away Safely." The violent will simply leave your world. They leave because they can't accept the truth.

401. Trust me! This is the most amazing story I have ever heard. Man must remember that God is his imagination and the powerhouse for the world. Your imagination holds infinite power. Imagine yourself in prison, but imagine being free. It doesn't matter how you get out. You will be able to recognize the infinite power within you when you see yourself in reality. You can imagine yourself being free. God will set you free.

402. The imaginative man doesn't deny the existence of the sensuous outer realm of Becoming. But he also knows that the inner world that is continuous Imagination is what brings the sensuous outer realm of Becoming to life.

403.   Who is Jesus Christ? Christ is the power of God and wisdom, and God gave himself to us. He became us so that we might live. . Like the earth . Wear out like a garment. Isaiah 51:6 tells us: "Lift your eyes up to the heavens and gaze at the earth below; for the heavens and earth will vanish as smoke, and the earth will wear like a garment, and those who live in it will also do the same; but my salvation and my deliverance will not be ended." The word "salvation," refers to Jesus. It is the salvation. This is eternal. It would not be that God became man so that man could become God. This is to save mankind and to lift them up to immortality.

404.   I have revealed the only source of all phenomena in life. It is important that you use it well.

405.   Scripture is all about you. You are the God-being, and you must claim it. You are the only power. Either you are conscious of your imagination or you will die in your sins. A physical man could not say, "Unless you believe in I AM He, you will die." He said these words: "I am from above." You come from below. You are from below.Your I AMness comes from above. After I have come to do the Father's will, I, who am now conscious of being you will

drink the cup to the end. However, no one can have any power over me except I, through my assumption, give them away. It is by making me believe I am less than others, and forcing him to play the role of someone superior to me. Everybody reflects my assumptions, and they play their part according to what I assume. For there is only Imagination and I AM He. If I'm afraid, then I live in fear. There is no other world. Protean means that I play every role in my life's dream, for my good and for my ill.

406.   God became man so that man might become God. What can I create in my transformation into man (as God is the only creator power in the universe)? My imagination. Although I might not be able to put it down on paper or execute it as well as artists, my imagination can still create it. I can picture a book, and the joy that comes with it. I can picture a picture. Even though I'm not an artist, I can still dream. It is impossible for me to imagine a painting that a man could paint on canvas that is more alive and vibrant than my dream. Yet, I can't even put anything on canvas. But when I go to bed, I can dream. What is causing it? My imagination. This is where I can dream, even though I have lost my conscious faculties. You can dream like no other artist; add color to it, motion on it and you will have the most amazing drama. . That is all I can think of.

407.   Wealth is a powerful tool, but it is only a small firecracker when compared to the power and imagination of Imagination. You can imagine any state you want, without any knowledge or background.

408.   I have seen scenes that are as real and solid as this one, and I know that if I arrest an activity within me everything will stop. After watching people eating, I realized that I had an activity in me. Everything stopped. Everything continues as it was intended when I release it. The world is a play that has been written. While the actors are only actors on stage, you can get so involved in the actions that you forget it is a play. His predetermined play is where imagination is buried, and he dies repeatedly until the Word that is buried with him awakens. This is God's awakening, and you are freed from the play. As the Psalms tell us, "To the Lord God belongs My redemption from Death." God doesn't redeem you from the outside. Every character   in

scripture is within you! All things are found in the Human Imagination which is the Divine Bodily!

409.   You may think someone is a rascal who takes what you have. But if you know that imagination creates reality, then you'll realize that you can't let anyone into your life without calling him. He could not have taken anything from you if you didn't call him. . Your attitude toward life . It was something I had allowed. You can either make the world your own or force it out. This is the story of scripture. Your amazing human imagination is the only God. When you speak of Jesus Christ, do you not mentally bow your head? If so, then you should do the same when you think about your imagination. The Word of God, imagining is God's own Word. Your amazing human imagination is what created the world. It supports and sustains it. Your imagination can change! You will experience a new world of happiness when you believe the change is possible.

410.   Trust me. Your only solid foundation is your imagination. This will allow you to experience a new freedom that you never knew before. It's a wonderful freedom! It's as easy as imagining! Imagination is the only foundation. Only Jesus Christ is the foundation that can be laid. There have been many attempts by man to build foundations in other isms. These are not Jesus Christ because he is man's I AMness, man's human imagination and there is no other God. Hear, Israel, the Lord, our God, the Lord, who is one and whose name forever is I AM! You will experience a new freedom when awareness is your way of living. You will realize that everything and everyone is you pushing out. As God, the father of all things, you will realize that even though it appears like everything is dying, they are not.Prayer is an art form that requires practice. Controlled imagination is the first requirement. Prayer is not able to tolerate parades or vain repetitions. It requires calmness and peace of mind.

412.   We are still here and we have a law that allows us to know God's identity through its operation. It is very simple. The law can be stated in many ways. One of them is "As a man seeds, so shall he reap." You are sowing the thought that you want to be the woman (or man) you envision. If you believe

that assumption, then you will see the fruits in your life. But first, you need to know what you want.

413.   Accept the challenge of Scripture and feel the desire to be fulfilled. . Not only for you, but also for your family members and friends. If you think for someone else, it is giving it to you. You are the only one who can push out the vastness of the universe.

414.   "The hour has arrived when the son of Man will be betrayed to the hands of sinners." The truth is that the human imagination is God. One billion people who claim to believe in Christ tonight will recoil from thinking that their human imagination could be God. They do not realize they are sinners and enemies of truth. The true Christ is God's wisdom and power housed in Man, as well as his wonderful human imagination. He would be destroyed by those who refuse to accept the truth and see only its manifestation. But he who recognizes the personification embraces them with open arms.

415.   Nothing that is perceived in perception cannot be duplicated in fancy. And what the world perceives is entirely imaginative. Let me give you an example. I'm sure that everyone has experienced the sensation of sensing the rose fragrance. Smell is a chemical sense that depends on contact to perceive. Is it necessary to smell a rose in order to recognize its scent? Its fragrance can be replicated imaginatively. Can you smell an Easter lily and not distinguish between the scents of a rose or a lily? They do not exist independently of you. Instead, they live on a level (or levels!) of your imagination!Do you have the ability to call on your memories of a long-gone experience, bring it back and create a duplicate in your imagination? This world is not unlike your imagination, if so, William Blake, in 1820, wrote "The Presence of The Divine Teacher" in which he stated: "Man is all imagination and God is Man and exists within us and in us." We are members of the Divine Body Jesus. Blake doesn't separate the members of the one body, the single spirit, one Lord and one faith from the Father. Only one Imaginal Body exists. We all are His members because we all are Imagination!

416.   The great and inspired poets are something I admire. Shakespeare is a marvel. Blakeis a marvellous man, and Einstein is truly a great scientist. They were both inspired men, but their spirit was not greater than yours. Their imagination and your imagination go hand in hand to create the world. Their creativity did not stem from anything outside themselves. It came from their own imagination and awakening. Because there is only one spirit, the same imagination can be yours. The spirit of man is one and the same with the spirit that is everywhere. There is no other spirit! Begin to feel this feeling. You will feel God and fall asleep. As you return from unconsciousness to this level, you will have many crazy dreams about this person.These dreams will be important to you. But, oh! What depths will you reach in the unconscious level relative to this level? Do not let anyone scare you. You are an immortal being that cannot die. I may have ascended to Godhood before you but that doesn't mean I am better. There is no such thing, being the first. Everybody is on the same path, and no one can stop them. When all are back, what joy! Everybody will see and be able to prove that he is God, the Father.

417.   This night, test your imagination and see if you can believe in the power of Christ. All things are possible for him. As you go about your day, you'll see how quickly you can achieve the world you want. One day, scripture will emerge in you, putting you in the center role. But in the meantime, you can choose what you want to do or be.

418.   Tonight, believe me. Your amazing human imagination is the one and only God. Let him know what you want, and he will make it happen. Find the feeling you want and search for it. Take a look at the world around you. . Would you see it differently? What would your friends and family think? Make that scene, feel the reality, and don't lose sight of it! Remember what you saw, how you felt. For he who creates in us must have a model. Do not be like Jesus, who said that the double-minded man was unstable in all his ways. He sees himself in the mirror of his life, and then he forgets who he really is. It is important to keep it in your heart and allow Christ the Lord (the one within you) to externalize it. You and He are one. You are not the Lord and I am not referring to you. You will one day discover that there is only God in the world.

419.   God is your amazing human imagination. He took on himself all the weaknesses and limitations of the flesh. . in turn . . You may be able to discover God, believe in yourself and apply your faith. One day, you will realize that God is all around you.

420.   Be careful about what you think. It will come to pass, no matter how small or trivial it may seem. The vastness of the world is only the product of our confused imaginations. It is possible that the world seems confused because man does not control his imagination. He believes he can think of anything without any restrictions, but he is not. All of it comes into the world to confront and show him his harvest. It was planted somewhere along the journey; now it is his harvest. He doesn't recognize his own. It is not easy to control your imagination day and night and steer the boat in the right direction. It must be done. Get started right away.

421.   Shadows will be fought by those who aren't awake, as imagination is all that's visible in this world. Shelley once stated:"He has woken from his dream of life.

We are the ones who get lost in stormy visions.

Combat phantoms, unprofitable strife and other evil forces."

People who fight against the establishment don't realize they are also fighting against the objectified images in their own minds. The day will come when the person who dreams his world will wake up and realize that he is the foundation of it, the one Jesus calls Jesus. The words "Jesus", "Joshua", and "Jehovah" refer to "Jehovah the Lord's salvation." Man is saved from his dreams by returning to the place he was in before the dream began.

422.   What is the best way to occupy a state? Ask yourself what you would do if you could live your dream. Set the stage. As the star of your production place yourself on the stage. Then, let a friend enter to see you in your new state. Write the script. . The words he would use to describe you when he meets you. Feel his touch. You can now embrace the new state that you've created in your imagination. It doesn't matter if anyone gives you permission. Simply imagine the state and then move into it until it becomes reality. Let the feeling take you to fulfillment.

423.   If you can imagine a state and remain faithful to it, then you have found the creator of the universe. Without imagination, nothing is made. You will find him when you learn how to make it. Moses and the prophets were inspired by your amazing human imagination.Sustainer of all life.

424.   Paul wrote to the Corinthians in his 1st letter. He said that "No other foundation can be laid than that which has been laid by Jesus Christ." In his second letter, he asked: "Does Jesus Christ not reside in you?" I now ask you: Who is this Jesus Christ who lives in you? He is your amazing human imagination. . Your world is built on your dreams! Your world is built on your dreams. The dreamer who dreams those dreams is Jesus Christ, which scripture refers to as your human imagination. While you may view Jesus as an outsider, as someone who is separate from you, I assure you that Jesus Christ is within you through your amazing human imagination. He is your dreamer, your foundation for your day and night dreams. Although you may not be able write, draw, or play a song, you can still dream because (Imagination Jesus Christ) is in you.

425.   Please believe me tonight. There is only one God, hewho is your amazing human imagination. If you turn to any other God, you will be a false God. Do not make a graven image of God. "I AM" does not have a face. The faces of Jesus have been drawn by unnumbered artists. He is just "I AM."

426.   I didn't know the story of Jesus Christ was my. I didn't know that Jesus understood the Old Testament with his own eyes; that it was the center of the human imagination. . our human I AMness . . He was. Now I am certain that there was never another Jesus, and there will never be another. Those who claim to teach another Jesus are teaching a false Christ.

427.   Don't believe that it won't happen because it doesn't seem possible. You can be confident that it will happen. Fame is what you need. You can also suggest to yourself that this is a time when you are awake and can see the frozen world. I hope that many of you will have the desire and courage to tell others what I'm doing. It is important that you first prove it to yourself. The art of repentance is a way to change your mind. You can do it again and again. It will prove that an inner change will bring about an outer change. It's possible to prove it, and then share your findings with others. Imagine the outcome you desire and keep at it until you see it. You will succeed no matter what your senses say. Remember that the body is only a garment, and you will eventually take it off. You are invisible and you can join the Divine Society to become one of Gods who create. You cannot fail when God is in you at all times.

428.   The outside world is a mirror of the dream man has, and he is searching for the savior who will change society and the establishment. The shadows will not conceal the existence of a savior. He can only be found in the midst of shadows if he is able to lay down within each individual man and awakens through a series of amazing events. You are the dreamer and the world is your dream. You can fight it if necessary. You can do whatever you want, but the dream will never end. You will then realize that you are the dreamer and creator of your dream. Your amazing human imagination is all that exists! There is no other God. There is no other Jesus Christ. There is no other God. Your imagination is the God of Scripture. This is what I have seen firsthand.

429.   You know the truth. Your imagination is more powerful than anything! He is the one who inspired Shakespeare, Einstein, and Blake. There is only one spirit in all of creation! Hear, O Israel! The Lord our God, God is One!" This one spirit is the human imagination. Blake was asked his opinion on Christ's divinity. He replied, "Christ is the only God. But so am I. So are you." Christ is not something you should consider greater than yourself. Christ is the only God. But so am I, and so are you. You are not less than Christ. There is only God. Your amazing human imagination is the only God. You can imagine all possible things. Now, you have to put this reality to the ultimate test. You may not believe it, but your rational mind and outer senses will. If you persist, you will get what you want. You are the same God that   created

and sustains all things. But you have been keyed down. If you want to make a difference, you need persistence.

430.   You can't see imagination, but you can see the fruits of imagination. Sono, no one has ever seen God because you are the reality known as "Imagination." You don't see imagination but you do see evidence. The fruit of imagination.

431.   "My every thought is a vibration that draws to me the meaning it is conveying." This was established from the beginning. "As a man sows so shall he reap." This is the law of identical harvest. It's also known as "seedtime" and "harvest" in scripture. There will be no changes. If you plant weal, you will reap it. The human imagination can make wheat grow. When you visualize, you vibrate and bring forth the things you've imagined. Your imagination is always present in the world. Although you may not be able to recognize your harvest or deny that you have ever thought such horrible thoughts, it is possible to prove it. You promised at the beginning that you would accept the consequences of any imaginal actions, whether they are good or bad. You can change the outside from now to the end of the time, but you cannot change your thinking. If you give a man anything on the outside, he will be conditioned by it. You can give him the gift of life by teaching him how to use his imagination and attract what he desires.

432.   This platform believes that God is all Imagination, and God isman (spiritual Man, not the skin he wears). Man is therefore all Imagination. We also believe that God is the only creator and God being human, we are creators. Life itself is an activity in Imagination. All of the world we live in is a world that's imaginable. We hope tonight to demonstrate it so that you can be inspired to take action and make it a reality. Everybody can be what they want to be. However, the true being of God is hidden and visible. Therefore, you cannot see its manifestation.

433.   You can achieve what you want in the world if you know your goals. Don't let anyone tell you that being acquisitive is a virtue. People who say that you are acquisitive would be happy to have the same thing as them. Be completely uninterested in the opinions of others and just go for it. You

can live a rich, full, and wonderful life if you know yourself. All you are is Imagination, and all of it is God. Only God creates.

434.   My experience has taught me that a false assumption can be made if it is persistently held. Continuous imagination is sufficient to accomplish all things. All my reasonable plans will not compensate for my lack of constant imagination.435. I asked myself many times: "If my imagination represents Christ Jesus and all things can be done to Christ Jesus, is all possible for me?"

436.   My experience has taught me that Christ (Imagination), awakens in me when I align myself with my goal in life. Christ (imagination), is enough for all things.

437. You are always thinking, no matter where you go. TheLord cannot be left behind. As much as the body can be wished away, you cannot just sit there and wish your imagination away. I can imagine myself standing at the other end of the room, and I can also imagine that I am looking at this particular one. But where are I? I am in imagination. The body is something I have left behind for a while. It is something I always return to. I cannot let go of my imagination. Because I am all imagination, I can't escape the Lord. If I can imagine feeling things the way I want them to be, it's the Lord doing it. Because "All things can be done by the Lord," I must believe that it is possible.438. The world is a revelation about the states with whom imagination is fused. The state we believe from determines what we see in the world.

439.   We need to use imagination well, not just as an observer thinkingoftheend, but as partakers thinkingfromtheend.

440.   You will soon stop fighting the shadows with your imagination. Your world will cease to be divided and you will find peace within yourself. Let those still asleep dream of violence in the world. It's fine, because in its

midst, you will be able to walk knowing that you are safe, since you are awake. This is your dream and it cannot be destroyed. Stop dreaming of violence and begin dreaming peace. . But not everyone will. They will instead call you crazy and say you are a devil, as they did with Jesus in scripture.

441.   Remember that perception cannot be duplicated in imagination. If you can perceive your desire, it exists. It is impossible to perceive something that doesn't exist at some level of your imagination. Your human imagination can be identified with God. God calls things that are not currently visible as though they were, so you can create a state by assuming you're there. If you believe that you have what you want, it will happen. You are looking at God instead of the devil if you use reason. The doubter within you is the devil. He will question your belief and say: "If You are the Son of God, then make this stone into bread." His angels will lift your spirits if you don't put your foot down. Self-doubt is the root of all these difficulties. You should practice the art and science of imagination. You will be able to prove your imagination in the test, even if you started off wrong!

442.   The Son of God is your wonderfulhuman imagination. Imagine is the very essence of life. When you visualize something, it becomes animated. It takes on motion and vibration.

443.   Any perception that you have experienced can be reproduced and duplicated in your imagination. You don't have to be present to think of a friend or loved one. You don't have to be present in your living space to view its contents. It doesn't matter if you are not there. You can see the Mississippi River, the mountains of Colorado and the plains of Kansas. This is why we can start from the idea of it as a world made up of imagination. It is He who creates reality. Fiction is not real in the truest sense of the term. A state that is imagined is created. Prayer is a state of being soaked in emotion. The feeling of fulfillment is what makes a desire manifest. This is something I know to be true. Regardless of what the rest of the world believes, reproduction in your mind can take on forms in your external world.

444.   Start now to use your imagination actively and continuously. As you prove its creative power on that level, you will be able to awaken to a higher level of consciousness and enter the spirit world where God is real. Feel

your desires are now a reality. Listen to what your friends have to say about you. Is it a celebration of your luck or envy? Imagine that their words are true. Keep believing that they are true. Keep believing that your dream is already a reality. When it is, you will have proof.Consider a gift you would love to give to someone. Ask yourself, if you were to give it to someone and he didn't like it, would it be something you would want to keep for yourself? For example, if you gave a million dollars to a friend and he refused, would you keep it? You would, I'm certain. Next, imagine that you are giving the money to him and then you will give it to others. Even if you don't have a bank account, you can still give because there is no one else to give to than yourself. Only God is known by the name I AM!

445.   It is the imagination that must be awakened.

446.   The birth of Christ (imagination), is demonstrated by man's ability to identify with his goal, even though reason and hissenses may deny it.

447.   The ultimate goal of imagination is to instill "the spirit Jesus" in us, which is continuous forgiveness of sins (always achieving our goal), constant identification of man with his ideal.

448.   Any place or state that we imagine, we will gravitate to it physically.

449.   One man can see where he is in his imagination.

450.   If you believe that imagination creates reality and practice repentance by radically changing your mind, then you can take any dissatisfying thing and make it work for you. You will then be convinced that the change is possible. You can expect it to conform to what you think, and the room, man, or woman will be able to witness your repentance. If you change your attitude toward another person, he will change his attitude towards yourself. We are often told that we love him because he first loves us. It all starts with you! You must make the change if you want him to be better. You are also practicing repentance. The time has come and the kingdom is yours. Now is the time to repent and believe in the gospel!

451.   Although the world may think of many gods, there is only one. This one is your amazing human imagination. Only one son is God's only son. When imagination awakens, God will reveal you as God. The same thing will happen again to another. . eventually, everyone will see the same child who will reveal God the Father. This world is a play. God's imagination transforms into human imagination when he inserts himself into olive, black, white, and red skins. Even though we may appear different, we will all see God's only son. . Proving that there is only one God. This play is intended to increase imagination's creative potential. We are now fragmented into many parts and are destined to be reunited with the One God, the Father of all.

452.   The churches teach that there is another person greater than you, but they also say that you will be condemned if you don't believe in me as He. . These words were spoken by the imagination of man! Because imagination is one and you cannot escape that oneness, think of no other. These words should be understood in the present tense in the first person. If you don't believe you are already what you desire to be, you will end up in hell. If you don't believe that you are only imagining, you will keep believing the same old belief and worship a God outside of yourself.

453.   God can do anything! You should not assume that someone who is wildly wealthy has an infusion of spirit different from yours. You can imagine wealth in a wittingly or unwittingly way, but it is possible to do it knowingly. He may lose his wealth if he doesn't know what he's doing. No matter your financial situation or wealth, I want you to take control of your wealth. If you want to return to your old state tomorrow, claim "I AM wealthy" because there is only one God. Because there is no other creator, he who creates poverty creates wealth.   .

454.   To use your creativity, you don't need to be a genius scholar. A so-called brilliant mind only believes in what is visible and physical. Therefore, imagining can't fulfill a desire. I am a master of imagination. I have created a scene that implied my desire and gave it all the natural qualities so it felt right. . Let it be. Just as I would plant a seed in the ground and then wait for it to mature, so my seed of my desire matured and became a reality in my life. You can imagine what you want. Be confident that you will get it. Go about your

daily business with patience and confidence knowing that your desires will come true. You can't wait to receive power from above, so use the law.

455.   We have all heard it said, "Oh, that's just hisimagination." Only his imagination. . The man's imagination is his own. Although no man can have too much imagination, few people are able to control their imagination. The imagination is indestructible. Its misuse is the worst nightmare. Every day, we see a stranger walking down the street, muttering to his self, engaging in imaginary arguments with someone else. He is arguing with vehemence or fear, and he doesn't realize that he is creating an unpleasant experience he will soon encounter. As imagination sees the world, it is real. Our daily lives are shaped by imaginations, not facts.The literal and exact minded live in a fictional world. Only imagination can bring back the Eden we have been driven from by experience. The sense that we perceive the above, and the power to bring it into existence is called imagination. The imagination is the key to every stage of man's development. Because men don't always see the whole picture, they believe their results may sometimes be uncertain. The beginning of any successful operation is determined imagination. Only the imagination can fulfill the intent. Because he can summon any image he wants, the man is most free to use his imagination. A solitary or captive can use his imagination and feelings to affect many people and speak through many different voices.

456. The imaginative man views the outer world and all its happenings in the light of his inner world of Imagination.

457.   The imaginative man recognizes that all men must be conscious of their inner activity and understand the relationship between the inner causality world of imagination, and the sensuous outer world effects.

458.   It's amazing to realize that you can place yourself in the state of your fulfillment and escape the prisons of ignorance.

459.   It seems insane to think that imagination creates reality. But every mystic knows that every natural result has a spiritual cause. It is impossible to see a natural cause. This is a delusion of the world. Man's memory is so poor that he can't relate what is happening now to an earlier imaginal act. Man is always looking for physical causality and cannot believe that he could have imagined such an effect. Yet, I can tell you this: Imagining something will set a cause into motion. You may not be able to see the effects, but you know your "now" is real and alive because of your imaginal actions. You may think that imagination is the cause of all things, but your memory is flawed. Therefore, you might view someone who claims that life is caused by imagination to be a fool. . Blake would still call you an idiot thinker and not a man with imagination.

460.   My belief is that every man can change the course of their lives, just like Dr. Millikan. To anyone seeking the truth, Dr. Millikan's method of making his wish a reality to himself is a great help. His high purpose is to make "mutual benefits" the goal for all of us. It's much easier to see the benefit of everyone than to think only for ourselves. We can change the world by using our imagination and affirming our beliefs. This is natural for the man of high purpose and the disciplined man. Let us all be disciplined.

461.   The 17th verse of the Book of Romans is the 4th Chapter. Paul says: "God calls those things that aren't seen as though they were visible, and the unseen becomes visible." How does he do this? It's through movement. When I move, all that was invisible becomes visible. You have spoken to me, and I can see you now. Although it is not visible, I can see your radiant smile because your desire has taken on substance and life. I have changed how I see you. If I change from what I am into what I want to be, you'll still be my friend. So in my imagination, I let you see me the way you would see me if things were like I imagine them to be. They are what I want them to be. And so I am. I cannot be blind and allow you to see me in my old state. But, I must continue in my new state until it is natural and out images itself in my world. I don't care about what you do. You will be known if you desire to be known. For your assumptions, simply assume you are. . Although you may deny it, . If you persist in this, it will become an externalized fact in your life.

462.   You can learn to live in your imagination every day, morning, noon, night. The gentleman whose stories I shared with him tonight said that he initially thought I was crazy when he heard me. But he tried it and it made sense. Although I understand that the law and the promise are not logical from a worldly perspective, I can tell you that there is a plan for redemption in you. You will be able to experience everything written about Jesus in scripture. You will then see that he wasn't a physical being but a name for a plan. Jesus is Jehovah. He is your wonderful I AM.

463.   Truth is dependent upon the intensity of imagination and not on external facts.

464.   The fruit bear witness to the misuse or use of theimagination.465. Man becomes what he imagines.

466.   Imagination is the key to the truth and the way to the light.

467. This power is called the law. Just decide what you want, and then imagine a scene that would make it seem like you have achieved it. Get into the spirit of the scene. Participate by adding sensory vividness to the scene.Relax and let it happen. Do not think about the ends. You are already living in your dream and it is now possible to realize it. Have faith. Faith is loyalty to your unseen reality. Although it is not visible, your imaginal act is real for God. You would answer "I AM" if I asked who is imagining it. God is God forever and ever.

468.   We discover, as we awaken to our imaginative lives, that to imagine something is to make it happen, and that true judgments need not be conformed to external realities.

469.   To make the future dream a reality, one must first imagine it. The reality we imagine in our imagination must be experienced in real life. It is never free from the outcome if it doesn't imagine itself in a situation.

470.   "Now is the time to make beauty out of ashes, to bring joy, to praise the spirit of heaviness, and to plant trees of righteousness for Him. Control your imagination and pay attention now. Control does not refer to restraint with will power, but cultivation through love and compassion. We cannot emphasize enough the power of imaginative love in a world that is so divided. I want to show you all the true meaning of Zechariah's words, "Speak ye to every man the truth to your neighbor and let no one imagine evil in their hearts against your neighbor." This is a great challenge for you and me. "A man thinks in his heart, so is he." He is what he imagines. Keep your love alive in your imagination. You can create an ideal in your mind until you are one with it. This will allow you to transform yourself or absorb its qualities into your very core. Never lose sight of the power within you. Imaginative love is a way to see the unseen and give us water in the desert. It is the only place that can give the soul its true home. The garden is full of beauty, love, and all good reports. However, imaginative love is the key to the garden.

471.   There is only one foundation. It is your wonderful humanimagination. Let me now tell you about another lady who is present tonight. She stated that her mother had told me ten days ago that she believed she was suffering from the same problem as she had a year earlier. I wrote to her immediately after I received the letter. She believed me so much that she read the letter and sent the results back to me. My family has never understood the meaning of the word "imagination", so I use the term "God" and they get it.

472.   Prayer is a controlled dream. To pray well, we must keep our eyes on the world in the same way that we would see it if our prayers were answered. Although it doesn't require any special faculties, steady attention does require control over imagination. Our senses must be expanded. . Take note of our new relationship with the world, and then trust our observations. It is possible to feel, touch, and sense the new world, but not to grasp it. It is best to be fully aware of it. We can also hear and see voices from within ourselves by listening to what we hear and looking like we saw. The outer world collapses when our attention is focused on the desired state. . Like music . All discords can be transformed into harmony by using a new setting.It is not about fighting but surrendering to life. The powers we invoke are more powerful than those we use to answer our prayers. The soul is not blind as

long as it takes notice. . The world that moves us is what we create, not what surrounds us. Our whole being must be open to the idea of becoming the noble person we desire to be. The prayer will be futile if anything is not granted. Our efforts to attain our highest goal often lead us to being denied our high goals. It is our responsibility to assume that we are already the man we want to be. This is possible if we are able to do it without effort. . We will find it by imagining in our imagination what we would feel in the flesh if we achieved our goal. Our attitude is the key to healing. Only our attitude can change. If you don't have it, imagine it. Pray for me; prayer can do more than the world imagines.

473.   The beginning of any magical operation is a controlled imagination and steady attention that are firmly and repeatedly focused on the idea being realized. He creates in himself a center for power if he perseveres through weeks and even months. He will travel a path that many may follow, but few others can. It is a path within him where his feet initially falter in darkness and shadow, but that is later made brighter by an inner light. It does not require any special talents or genius. It can be won through persistence and meditation. He will persevere and the dark caverns in his brain will become luminous. He will continue to set aside an hour for meditation every day as if he were making a date with a loved one. He feels like a diver who has spent too much time under water. When the moment arrives, he begins to feel the air and the light. He experiences in this meditative state what he would in real life if he had realized his goal.

474.   You are free as the wind! You can live a life of blissful imagination. You will know that you are the God who created the world and sustains it without losing your identity. You will realize that you didn't start when you arrived here. Instead, you have been traveling for many centuries. You've done terrible and violent things, but God in infinite mercy has erased them from your memory so you can live with yourself. All of your past will be forgotten when God comes to you with the eternal history and salvation. It will all be erased as if it never existed. You will be forgiven and forget all the horrors that you experienced in this time. All things have a beginning and an end. But there is no beginning or end to eternity. It is what it is! It was not

God who created the history of Salvation. It was always so. It was His plan that He would insert Himself into time to redeem humanity!

475.   Truth is an ever-increasing source of illumination. Anyone who seeks truth honestly does not need to be afraid of the result. Every raising truth brings out a larger truth that it had concealed. True seekers of truth are not arrogant, critical, or holier than thou. The true seeker of truth is not a smug, critical, or holier than thou person. "Speak to every man the truth and don't imagine anything evil against your neighbor." Truth seeker does not judge by appearances. . He sees the goodness and truth in everything he observes. He understands that true judgment does not have to conform to the external reality it is referring to. We are never so blind to the truth when we see things as they appear to be.Only images that are idealized can really represent the truth. It is not superior insight, but rather purblindness. This blindness can read into the greatness and smallness of another person. Everybody knows at least one gossipy petty who imagines evil and spreads it far and wide. He always adds, "It's fact," or "I know the truth" to his cruel accusations. He is so far from the truth. It doesn't matter if he knew the truth. But it's better to not say it. "A truth told with bad intention beats all lies you can create." This man does not seek the truth as it is revealed in the Bible. He does not seek truth, but only support for his view. He opens the door to his enemies and allows them access to his secret places. Let's seek the truth, as Robert Browning says: "Truth is in us; it takes no rise from outward things.

All of us have an eternal center where truth is in its fullness. The imaginative love that governs the truth within us is what is called the truth. This great truth means that we cannot imagine any evil against our neighbor. We will see the best in our neighbor.

476.   All people have an instinctive desire to do the loving thing. We can only do the loving thing if all that we see is filled with love for our neighbor. Only then can we see the truth, which is the truth that frees all people. This is my belief that this message will help us all live a more fulfilling

and satisfying life. God, the Father, was the name given to infinite love that had an unimaginable source. God, the Son was called infinite love in creative expression. Infinite love was described as God, the Holy Spirit. It is important to learn to see ourselves as Infinite love, and as good instead of evil. This is not something we need to be, but rather something we can recognize as we are. Love is the original place where imagination was born. Its lifeblood is love. Its visions are images that reflect truth, as long as it retains its own blood.It then mirrors the living identity it sees. If imagination denies the power that brought it into being, then the worst kind of horror will ensue. Instead of bringing back the living images of truth, imagination will fly towards love's opposite. . Fear and its visions will be perverted, and their reflections cast on a screen filled with frightful fantasy. It will no longer be the creative force that is supremely creative, but it will be the active agent for destruction. If man has a truly imaginative attitude towards life, God and man are one creative entity. Remember that Love is creative and causative in all spheres, from the highest to lowest.

It has never existed a thought, word, or deed that wasn't caused by love or its opposite. . Fear of any kind is a good thing, even if it's a wish for a less worthy goal. Fear and love are the foundation of our mental machinery. Before anything becomes a thing, it is only a thought. To make it a reality of being, I recommend that you pursue a high ideal. This can be done by training your imagination to see that Infinite Love is the only environment in which we truly live, move, and have our being. God is love. Love never fails. The infinite creative spirit of love is the Infinite. Love is the impulse that caused infinite unconditioned consciousness to become millions of sensitive forms.

477.   We can experience the abundant life Christ promised us, but only when we feel Christ in our imaginations can we actually experience it.

478.   Imagination is our redeemer.

479.   Creativity is not an act or will but a deeper sense of receptiveness.
. Suceptibility to akeener. Acceptance of the End . Acceptance of the answered prayer . Find the means to realize it. Until the state of the answered prayers fills your mind, you can feel it until it takes over all other states. We must not work towards the development of our will but for the education of imagination and steadying our attention. Conflict can be avoided when prayer is successful. Prayer is above all else, simple. The greatest enemy of prayer is the effort. Only the most gentle will allow the mighty to surrender fully. Although the wealth of Heaven cannot be taken by strong wills, it can be given as a free gift to the God-spent moment. You can travel both spiritually and physically by following the principle of least resistance. It is important to assume that all we want is already within us. It just needs to be claimed. It is necessary to claim it in order to realize our dreams. If we believe that our prayers have been answered, then we can continue to assume that the wish has been fulfilled.480 . That is, they have faith in their imagination?

481. Isn't the promise Believe you will receive and you will receive the same as "Imagine you are and you will be"?

482.   Let's be mindful of our emotions, our reactions to the events of the day. Let us guard our feelings more diligently in prayer. Prayer is the true creative state. Dignity is when man listens to the greater music of his life and follows the rhythm of its deeper meaning. The world would be transformed if we only imagined and felt the beautiful. Many stories in the Bible focus on the power of imagination, feeling, and many others. The cry of truth seekers is "Feeling for Him". Only imagination and feeling will restore the Eden we have been driven to by experience. Imagination and feeling are the senses that allow us to see the beyond.They begin where knowledge ends. Every noble feeling in man is the doorway to the divine realm. We should not measure men by their heights, but rather by their imaginations, and their feelings. Let's take our thoughts to Heaven and combine our imagination with the angels. It is not the real world around us that makes us move, but the world we create. The unexplored continents and man's great future adventures are all within our imagination. All God-ward believers have experienced this awareness of non-finality when "feeling after God".

They realize that their conception of the Infinite has constantly deepened and expanded with experience. Those who endeavor to think out the meaning of the experience and to coordinate it with the rest of our knowledge, are the philosophic mystics; those who try to develop the faculty in themselves, and to deepen the experience are the practical or experimental mystics. Some, and among them the greatest, have tried to do both. Religion begins in subjective experience. Religion is what a man does with his solitude, for in solitude we are compelled to subjective experience.

483.   Even though you once considered Christ as human, when he isquickened in you, you will regard him thus no longer and speak out. You will be bold and tell everyone that their human imagination is the only creative power in the world. That God is imagination. He is the Father of all life. Imagining is his son, his creative power, and that is Jesus Christ.

484.   Any kind of meditation in which we withdraw into ourselves withoutmaking too much effort to think is an outcropping of the subconscious. Think of the subconscious as a tide which ebbs and flows. In sleep, it is a flood tide, while at moments of full wakefulness, the tide is at its lowest ebb. Between these two extremes are any number of intermediary levels. When we are drowsy, dreamy, lulled in gentle reverie, the tide is high. The more wakeful and alert we become, the lower the tide sinks. The highest tide compatible with the conscious direction of our thoughts occurs just before we fall asleep and just after we wake. An easy way to create this passive state is to relax in a comfortable chair or on a bed. Close your eyes and imagine that you are sleepy, so sleepy, so very sleepy. Act precisely as though you were going to take a siesta. In so doing, you allow the subconscious tide to rise to sufficient height to make your particular assumption effective.

When you first attempt this, you may find that all sorts of counterthoughts try to distract you, but if you persist, you will achieve a passive state. When this passive state is reached, think only on "things of good report" . . imagine that you are now expressing your highest ideal, not how you will express it, but simply feel HERE AND NOW that you are the noble one you desire to be.

You are it now. Call your high ideal into being by imagining and feeling you are it now.

485.   There is only one body. Everyone who awakes is incorporated intothat universal body to know you are it. And while your physical body sleeps, you will be all over the world. Your voice will be heard and you will be seen. That is the being you become after you have awakened from the dream of life. Tonight I urge you all to use the word imagination, for I have come to set this new idea against the old. Although people may rebel, when you get the results you want, it doesn't matter how they object. The term to be used now is your own wonderful human imagination

486.   This creative power is buried in everyone, and that power is Godhimself. There is no intermediary between you and God. Jesus Christ is the creative power of your own wonderful human imagination! That is Jesus Christ and there is no other! God the Father is buried in you as your I AM, and your human I AMness is Jesus Christ. This is the being Paul speaks of when he says: "Test yourself; Do you not realize that Jesus Christ is in you? Unless, of course, you fail to meet the test." Now let me share a letter from a friend. She said: "I am a freelance designer. I never seek work, but as I sit at home and imagine I am working, they call. In the past six months I have received very few orders from a company that kept me very busy in the past, so I called them to discover that they had employed a full-time art director and would no longer require my services.

After hanging up the phone I revised this conversation. I heard them tell me they had lots of work for me, and I felt the thrill in their words. One week later they called, asking me to design a 26-page book of institutional advertising, plus four ads for Harper's Bazaar. This was more than they had given me in the past at any one time. Now I am busier, happier, and making more money than ever before, and my technique is simple. Sitting in my chair I quietly listen for the phone to ring, answer it in my imagination and hear the orders I desire to create . . and they come."

487.   The best defense against the deceptive assault upon our mental andmoral eyesight is the spiritual eye or the Eye of God. In other words, a spiritual ideal that cannot be changed by circumstance, a code of personal

honor and integrity in ourselves and good will and love to others. "Not what thou art, nor what thou hast been, beholdeth God with his merciful eyes, but that thou wouldst be." Through the veins of the humblest man on earth runs the royal blood of being. Therefore, let us look at man through the eyes of imaginative love which is really seeing with the Eye of God. Under the influence of the Eye of God, the ideal rises up out of the actual as water is etherealized by the sun into the imagery cloudland.

Things altogether distant are present to the spiritual eye. The Eye of God makes the future dream a present fact. Not four months to harvest . . look again, If we persist in this seeing, one day we will arise with the distance in our eyes, and all the staying, stagnant nearby will suddenly be of no importance. We will brush it aside as we pass on to our far-seen objective. The man who really finds himself cannot do otherwise than let himself be guided by love. He is of too pure eyes to behold iniquity. Our ability to help others will be in proportion to our ability to control and help ourselves. The day a man achieves victory over himself, history will discover that to have been a victory over his enemy. The healing touch is in an attitude, and one day man will discover that one governs souls only with serenity. The mighty surrenders itself fully only to the most gentle.

488.   Having imagined what you want in the world, if doubt appears inthought or personified by another, say to yourself: "Get thee behind me Satan (get out of my sight) . . I will have nothing to do with you."

489.   Discouraged people are sorely in need of the inspiration of greatprinciples. We must get back to first principles if we are to speak with a voice that will kindle the imagination and rouse the spirit. Again, I must repeat, in the creation of a new way of life, we must begin at the very beginning with our own individual regeneration. Man's chief delusion is his conviction that he can do anything. Everyone thinks he can do . . everyone wants to do and all ask, "What to do?" What to do? It is impossible to do anything. One must be. It is hard for us to accept the fact that "We, of ourselves, do nothing." It is especially difficult because it is the truth and the truth is always difficult for man to accept. But, actually, nobody can do anything.

Everything happens . . all that befalls man . . all that is done by him . . all that comes from him . . all this happens, and it happens in exactly the same way that rain falls . . as a result of a change in the temperature in the higher regions of the atmosphere. This is a challenge to us all. What concept are we holding of ourselves in the higher regions of our soul? Everything depends upon man's attitude towards himself. That which he will not affirm as true within himself can never develop in his world. A change of concept of self is the right adjustment . . the new relationship between the surface and the depth of man. Deepening is, in principle, always possible, for the ultimate depth lives in everyone, and it is only a question of becoming conscious of it.

Life demands of us the willingness to die and to be born again. This is not meant that we die in the flesh. We die in the spirit of the old man to become the new man, then we see the new man in the flesh. "Subjection to the will of God" is an old phrase for it and there is, I believe, no new one that is better. In that self-committal to the ideal we desire to express, all conflict is dispersed and we are transformed into the image of the ideal in whom we rest. We are told that the man without a wedding garment reaches the Kingdom by cleverly pretending. He does not believe internally what he practices externally. He appears good, kind, charitable. He uses the right words, but inwardly he believes nothing. Coming into the strong light of those far more conscious than himself, he ceases to deceive.

A wedding garment signifies a desire for union. He has no desire to unite with what he teaches, even if what he teaches is the truth. Therefore, he has no wedding garment. When we are united with the truth, then we will put off the old nature and be renewed in the spirit of our mind. Truth will strip the clever pretenders of their false aristocracy. Truth, in its turn, will be conquered and governed by the aristocracy of goodness, the only unconquerable thing in the world.

490.   Do not look for any physical causation, for causation is invisible.The world is all imagination, as you imagine you are Jesus Christ. Do you believe in your imaginal act? On this level the made reveals the mistakes of the maker. Learn from your mistakes. In a moment of anxiety perhaps you made that which you do not want. Learn from that which you made, where you made your mistake. Don't deny your harvest. Reap it, then plow and plant

again, this time in the moment of joy and thanksgiving. Learn to believe in your own wonderful human imagination. There is nothing in the world but God and his creative power. God needs no intermediary between you and himself because he is buried in you. Learn to trust this creative power in you and then God will reveal himself to you.

491.   If anyone ever asks you what you think of Christ, tell them that he isyour own wonderful human imagination; that he became you, with all of your weaknesses and limitations, that you may be God the Father. May I tell you: when you really believe this your outer world will change to conform to the inner changes that radiate from you. Your world is forever mirroring and reflecting all of your beliefs, so any modification of a belief will cause a change in your outer world. So instead of working on little things like wealth, health, and fame, work on the major concepts of Christ by learning to know him through exercising your own wonderful human imagination.

492.   Not everyone sought Christ. Some found him and brought others. Inthe Book of John we are told that Andrew found his imagination to be Jesus and told his brother Peter. Philip found him and brought his friend Nathaniel. Peter and Nathaniel were not seekers, but were introduced to the truth. And who did they find? The one of whom Moses and the law and the prophets spoke, Jesus of Nazareth. Where is he? Come and you will see that the drama is supernatural. Having heard the truth from one who has experienced it, do you reject my words or do you accept them? If you accept my words and toy with this idea to the degree that you become enamored, you will modify your former belief concerning Christ Jesus. Tonight one billion believe in a little personal being who walked the earth 2,000 years ago, because they do not understand the concept that is the vision of Jesus Christ.

493.   I ask you to believe me, for "Unless you believe that I AM He youwill die in your sins." You will miss the mark and never reach your goal unless you believe that you are right now the man you want to be. Is happiness your goal? Then assume it, for unless you assume "I AM happy," you will remain unhappy. You want to be secure? Then assume "I AM secure." That is the only way you will attain it. I AM Imagination, the only power in the world, for Imagination is God. Unless I imagine I AM the man I want to be, I will continue to imagine I am the man I do not want to be. No power on the

outside can make me other than what I think I AM. I must assume my own divinity, and as I do it will unfold within me.

494.   I do not care what the world will tell you, imagination creates itsreality. All of these precepts must be accepted literally, for they are literally true. What person truly believes that he was born to be what he is today? He may have been born into a family of great wealth, and . . being surrounded by it . . he takes wealth for granted; but that is an assumption. He may even believe he is entitled to it; but if you checked into his family tree, you would discover that his father or grandfather had a vision which became his reality. And if he who was born into wealth does not know the principle that supports it, he can lose the money and never regain it again. But you who know that everything is based upon an assumption realize that no one can take anything from you that you really want!

495.   Believe me. Dwell upon my words, for as you do the visions willunfold; and as far as your outer world is concerned you will never have to question what you shall eat or drink or wear, for you will have no need to be concerned about the marginal things of life. Start now to center your focus on Imagination and don't be concerned about the fringe. Seek the kingdom of heaven by turning your thoughts inward, and wonderful things will appear to come out of the nowhere. In my own case I never thought of or contributed to any money my parents made, yet when my father made up his will, all ten children shared equally. So while I was about my Father's business, completely absorbed in the kingdom of heaven and not concerned with dollars and cents, money grew in a foreign field. I had no knowledge or concern for its growth. Trusting my brothers implicitly, I have never once entertained the thought that anyone would ever take advantage of me, and no one has.

496.   From this platform I teach that I and my Father are one. Being one,my Father can never be so far off as even to be near, for nearness implies separation. What is there in you that can't even be near? Imagination! You cannot separate yourself from imagination. You can't claim: "I AM" and point to it as something on the outside. It is impossible to separate yourself from the sense of being, so in the sense of I AMness, you are imagining. If this sense

of oneness is your Father, do you really believe in him? If so, to what extent does your confession in words conform to your deep, deep conviction?

497.   Feeling is the secret of successful prayer, for in prayer, we feelourselves into the situation of the answered prayer and, then, we live and act upon that conviction. Feeling after Him, as the Bible suggests, is a gradual unfolding of the soul's hidden capacities. Feeling yields in importance to no other. It is the ferment without which no creation is possible. All forms of creative imagination imply elements of feeling. All emotional dispositions whatever may influence the creative imagination. Feeling after Him has no finality. It is an acquisition, increasing in proportion to receptivity, which has not and never will have finality.

An idea which is only an idea produces nothing and does nothing. It acts only if it is felt, if it is accompanied by effective feeling. Somewhere within the soul there is a mood which, if found, means wealth, health, happiness to us. The creative desire is innate in man. His whole happiness is involved in this impulse to create. Because men do not perfectly "feel," the results of their prayers are unsure, when they might be perfectly sure.

498.   Blake, claiming that his great poem "Jerusalem" was dictated fromon high, stated: "All that you behold, though it appears without, it is within, in your Imagination of which this world of mortality is but a shadow." Blake meant us to take that statement literally. All that you are conscious of is within you. Where else could it be? Looking out, and seeing this world as mechanical and not spiritual, causes you to remain lost in your search, for the world is your mirror. You are its source. Everything you perceive is within, for it is in the head that God created the heavens and the earth. I am not speaking of your mortal head. It is only a symbol, a reflection of your immortal one.

The day will come when your mortal head will return to dust, but there is a head that survives this one. A head capable of instantly restoring and clothing you in a mortal frame just like your present one . . only young . . to find yourself in a terrestrial world just like this. That is the head in which God sleeps. It is there that the pattern is buried. And it is in that head that the pattern man unfolds to reveal you as the source. Man finds it difficult to believe he is the cause of all life, yet I say there is no other. Look into the eye of your friend . . or enemy . . and you will see only yourself.

499.   We are told that whatever we desire, when we believe we alreadyhave received it, we will. This promise is based upon the premise that imagining creates reality. There is nothing you cannot become or have as an objective fact, if you believe you already have it. No restriction or condition has been placed upon the power of belief. If you will deny the evidence of your senses, suspend your reason, and persuade yourself that you are now the person you want to be, you will become it! Ask yourself how your friends would see you if you now embodied the idea you desire. Your true friends would rejoice, would they not? Then, if this statement is true, all you have to do is persist in believing your assumption is true, and it will harden into fact.

500.   Now, in the earliest gospel, the Gospel of Mark, we find thesewords: "The time is fulfilled and the kingdom of heaven is at hand; repent and believe in the gospel." The word "repent" means "a radical change of attitude (of thinking) towards anything that you either dislike or want to change." A radical change on your part will produce a corresponding change in your outer world. So now you are urged to examine yourself to see whether you are holding to the faith. Are you accepting as facts the headlines you see in the paper? The telephone call you just received! The morning's mail or the news on TV which suggest unlovely, horrible things to you? A friend calls, and pouring out all the bilge in the world tells you how bad things are and how they are destined to get worse. As you listen, their woes enter and are assumed by you. Now, if you understand this law that imaging creates reality, you should, like a computer, choose what you are going to allow to enter. And when the conversation is finished and your friend's voice is still fresh and clear in your ear, hear her changed words, the changed tone of her voice, and feel the joy emitted there.

QUOTES 501 - 600

501.   "Every natural effect has a spiritual cause, and not a natural. Anatural cause only seems. It is a delusion of the perishing vegetable memory." (Blake, from "Milton") If man could only bear in mind that every simple little imaginal act sends a quiver through Omniscience, right through

Omnipotence, and right through Immanence so the whole thing is like a huge, big computer, . . your imaginal act instantly is added to the sum total of it all; and instantly the whole. thing is changed, and the world is reflecting every imaginal act in this world of man, and keeping it all perfectly recorded, so that there is no such thing as a natural cause. It is all a spiritual cause. "All things were made by Him, and without Him was not anything made that was made." And where does He dwell? He dwells in us, for He is Spirit, and "the Spirit of God dwells in us." He dwells in us, and I have, by experiment, discovered what that Spirit is; and I tell you from my own experience, the Spirit of God and the human imagination are one. They are not two. So when you depart this world, your reality . . which is the Spirit of God . . is your own wonderful human imagination; and that gives cubic reality to everything in this world if you enter it. Now, the secret is to enter it. Can I enter the state of my wish fulfilled? Those other states were simply experiments. Can I enter the state of the wish fulfilled? I have done it. On several occasions I have. When it seemed essential, I did it. If someone asked of me, I tried my best to do it. And how do I do it? By feeling.

502.   The story recorded in the Old Testament lays the foundation ofwhich the New Testament is its fulfillment, but "Even to this day when Moses is read a veil is over their minds and they cannot understand it." When the mind is veiled, one cannot understand that the God spoken of by the prophets is imagination; but I tell you: at night when you go to bed God is dreaming, and when you awake in the morning he is still dreaming your world into being.

503.   We have been talking about God's law and God's promise. God'slaw is conditional. You cannot be in one state and not suffer the consequences of not being in another state, and you and I are free to imagine any state in the world, and imagining that state we can occupy it. Occupying the state, we fertilize it; having fertilized it, it has its own appointed hour for fulfillment. Every vision has its own appointed hour it will flower; if it seems long, wait for it . . it is sure and it will not be late. Some things will grow overnight, and some things will grow in a week, then in three weeks, and then in a month, and some things will take years. It could be a problem over which we seem to have no control. We have told you the story here, where on one occasion it took five years, but oh! the joy of reaping the fruit then. It was the

relationship of a mother and son-in-law. I have told you unnumbered stories where it took intervals of time, but it doesn't matter, if we apply the principle.

504.   Grant to everyone the good he asks of you, without putting yourhand in your pocket. Grant it by an imaginal act on your part. Try to be as faithful as you can to that imaginal act; believe in the creativity of that imaginal act, and as you do it, they will all become the embodiment of what they asked of you.

505.   "I, even I, am He, and there is no God beside me. I kill, and I makealive; I wound, and I heal; and none can deliver out of my hands." And the God spoken of in that chapter is seated here in everyone who is seated, for that one in you is the Spirit of God, and the Spirit of God is your own wonderful human imagination. So blame no one in this world for anything that befalls you.

506.   Right now you can use your powerful imagination to assume you arewhat at the moment your senses and reason deny. Walk in this assumption, knowing you are all imagination, and all things are possible to you. Dare to believe in the reality of your assumption and watch the world play its part relative to its fulfillment. Your assumption may appear to be false when first imagined; but if you will persist, it will harden into fact, because God is he who is doing the assuming. All of the objective facts you see here on earth are only shadows, which fade because imagination is their reality.

507.   This platform is concerned only with the great secret of life. Here weare convinced that the Supreme Power that created and sustains the universe is Divine Imagining, and it does not differ from human imagination save in degree of intensity. So God-in-man is your wonderful Imagination; that is God. We tell you that Imagination creates Reality, but bear in mind that at this human level on earth it takes time and persistence. If we will persist in the image, live in it, sleep in it, breathe in it, it will crystallize into tangible form. Night after night we take different facets of this truly great secret, and as we turn to the greatest book on Imagination in the world, we treat it differently. So, as we turn to it, bear in mind that the Bible is addressed to the Imagination, not to the man of sense or the man of reason . . the one that is "lost" or "dead" or "sound asleep."

508.   Whatever your inspiration may be, you will draw to yourself thatwhich you have assumed you want to be. If in your mind's eye a certain person is great and you want to be as great as he is, you will draw him out of yourself to instruct you. You are only instructing yourself, however, for every vision takes place within the human imagination. "All that you behold, though it appears without, it is within your imagination of which this world of mortality is but a shadow." Choose an image you would like to express. Feel you are that image. So appropriate it that it must come forth in your world of shadows. Do that and you are praying, for prayer is your own wonderful human imagination, drenched with feeling.

509.   God is real. You may not question it . . I don't . . but in 1963, thescientific world would question it. I don't know all the uses of the word, "God," but I like it. But if it will help you any, I use the word I use most: "imagination," because to me when I think of God I mean the same as when I say "divine imagination." When I speak of Christ I mean divine imagining, God in action. We are told: "God is Christ reconciling the world to himself." Imagining is Christ, which is God in action. So imagination in Christ with his imagination, imagining, is reconciling the whole vast world to himself. But if it offends you, go back to the word, "God," but don't put God on the outside of something separated from you, because he is not.

510.   The most creative thing in us is to believe a thing into objectiveexistence. Can you believe that something is already objective to you, even though your mortal eyes cannot see it? Can you walk, drenched in the feeling that it is an objective fact, until it becomes so? That's how everything is brought into being, for all things exist in the human imagination, who is God himself. Imagination is the divine body called Jesus, the Lord. If you are willing to step out, asking no one if it is right or wrong, and dare to walk in the assumption your image is true, it will come to pass.

511.   Let me define Imagination for you. It is spiritual sensation, but theword "spiritual" is to most of us something that is not practical . . the incorporeal as opposed to the corporeal. But Imagination is the power to perceive what is absent from the senses. Take a rose . . there is not one here . . but right now could I sense it in any way? Smell it? Touch it? I can, though it is absent from the senses. That is Imagination. If Imagination creates reality,

such perception of what is absent from the senses makes it so. We have unnumbered case histories to prove it. Imagination is the power to perceive what is absent from the senses, and if you persist, you go beyond the sense man and go beyond the rational man. "The natural man receives not the things of the spirit of God for they are foolishness unto him."

512.   God's revealed name to this world is "I AM." That is his great name.Can you say, "I AM?" That is God. What am I doing? I am thinking you are no good . . well, that is what you're doing, that is God in action. And do you know: you will live to see the day you are right. So "I AM" doing what? Anything in this world, all things are possible to God. When you say: "I don't believe so and so." Perfectly all right, that's your privilege, but who is not believing it? "I AM," you say . . well, that is God. Don't believe it. "I am no good, I can't make a living." Well that is your privilege; believe it and may I tell you how true God is: he'll prove it. Finally you are relieved and you will say to me: "I told you it's no good." Can't you realize that you are setting it in motion and you were fertilizing it in your world, for God's only revealed name is "I AM." So, what are you imagining?

513.   Ask yourself: "If I now believe that I AM He that the worldworships as the Lord, and all things are possible to me, then I must test myself and according to my faith in myself will it be done unto me." It is up to the individual to perform the action, for the evidence always follows the action. Act as though things are as you would like them to be. Persuade yourself that it is true and let the results follow. This is how you are called upon to operate in this world. This is imagination. It is not written in detail, but only sketches that you fill in with your life.

514.   Start examining yourself. Do you believe that imagining createsreality? If you do, then test yourself. Do you not realize that Jesus Christ (imagination) is in you? Do you have the courage to claim; "I AM He and besides me there is no other?" In the 8th chapter of John, the statement is made: "You will die in your sins unless you believe that I AM He." This is not a statement of another telling you that you must believe he is God. No! You are forever talking to yourself! Limited by the five senses, "I" . . Christ (Imagination) in you . . will miss my goals in life unless "I" believe that "I AM" that which "I" formerly desired to be.

515.   Everyone will fulfill scripture, for life is not finished until thishappens. No man is going to come from outer space, or from some holy womb, and save you! Christ (imagination) comes to you from within you, because that is where he is buried. Your body is his sepulcher, from which he rises and unfolds. And only when this happens will you know the truth and be set free. Now, you either believe me, and use your imagination . . consciously, or you do not. If you do not act now, you will eventually, as no one will be lost. If you die tonight your belief will not be transformed, but you will be restored to life in a world just as real as this one. You will know the same limitations as you know here. You will suffer, be deceived, betray and be betrayed, until you believe to the point of action. Then scripture will unfold within you, and you will depart this age of death to enter the age of life by controlling your own wonderful human imagination.

516.   The average person, believing only that which can be seen andtouched physically is real, will think I am crazy. A very intelligent, wonderful man who attended my meetings in New York City, once told me he enjoyed listening to my words; but when he did, he planted his feet into the carpet and held the sides of the chair to remind himself of the reality and profundity of things. Otherwise he would take off into some dream world. Call it a dream world if you will, but if there is evidence for a thing, does it matter what others think? I had evidence for my belief and I tried to share my experiences with him, but he would not even test his imagination. Not everyone who hears the truth will believe it, even though he seems to be so wise in the eyes of the world. So I say: I have yet many things to say to you, but you cannot hear them now. I am not speaking of the law. Mark puts that quite simply: "Whatever you desire, believe you have received it and you will." I am speaking of the promise and urge you to search the scriptures, for if you do you will find me there. And when you find me, you will know, from experience that you and I are one.

517.   If you will but control what you are imagining, not a thing isimpossible to you. And you will discover that when you find God, your values change. You will no longer worship things, rather you will worship God, the creator of the things. It is so thrilling to imagine something for a friend and watch it come into being, then to give thanks to the one who did it within you. When you thank God, you worship God and serve God. When your   friend

gives you the good news that he has what you had imagined for him, thank him for telling you; but your real thanks will go to God, for . . having found him, you now honor him, knowing he will never let you down. You don't have to burst a blood vessel when you imagine. Just let it be so. Knowing your request is genuine, imagine it as already accomplished and then trust him implicitly. This has nothing to do with any moral or ethical code, but your trust in God. Knowing that when you imagine, God is acting and God is faith, trust him to bring it to pass for he will, and in a way you could never devise.

518.   As we are told, "Do you not realize that Jesus Christ (imagination) isin you?" Then test yourselves to see if you really realize it. Put yourself to the test If I say, "Jesus Christ," and your mind jumps on the outside to something other than yourself, you have failed the test, for you are told: "Do you not realize that Jesus Christ is in you? . . unless, of course," said he, "you fail to meet the test!" Well, you have just had the test. So, when I use the words, "Jesus Christ," and something on the outside comes to you, you have failed the test!, for Jesus Christ is in you. If I go to Him in my prayer, where would I go but to myself? He became as I AM, that I may be as He is. He actually became me. He is in me as my own wonderful human imagination, for "by Him all things were made, and without Him was not anything made that was made," so I go within and appropriate the state.

So, the subjective appropriation of my objective hope is my prayer. And having appropriated it, I drop it, as I would the seed into the earth. The seed must fall into the earth and rot before it can be made alive. Well, just drop it, and then in its own good time it will come into harvest. It takes an interval of time between my appropriation and its fulfillment; so having done it, I drop it, and go about my "Father's business" appropriating other states . . not only for myself, but for myself pushed out," which I call "others." For, in the end, there is Only One.

519.   Your imagination is the true vine from which everything in yourworld is drawn. Any misuse of your imagination causes the deformities in your life. It is a shock, I know, to realize that you are the sole cause of your life; and what a responsibility you have, to prune this true vine of awareness! Since the Father and the Son are one, I . . as Father AM the true vine and must prune myself. Not realizing a seeming other was a branch growing from me,

the true vine, I allowed myself to entertain unlovely thoughts of him. But I didn't cut the branch, for the pruning is not in that way. Called repentance in scripture, pruning is revision . . which is a radical change of attitude towards an individual or a situation. I revised my thoughts relative to that seeming other and accepted this unseen imaginal act as reality. Then I watched, and in time I became aware of a change in my world relative to this person or that condition. Having found the true vine and the Father who pruned it, I know I must prune it every day; for if I do it will knot and form itself into these full, clean clusters to repay the hand of the vinedresser (the Father) who pruned it.

520.   Anything is possible if you can feel it; but if you are going to usereason it will never happen, because failure becomes your image. You don't realize it but there are two of you, and it is your deeper self that tells you it can't happen. But no real belief can ever be suppressed for long, for your inward conviction (Imagination) must find some external objective habitation, and it will.

521.   I tell you: the only God in the universe is your own wonderfulhuman imagination. When you say: "I AM," that is God. There is no other God other than he who is encased in the limitation of your little garment of flesh. How can you call upon him, when you do not believe you are he? And how can you believe in him of whom you have never heard? What preacher ever told you that your own wonderful human imagination is God? They paint a word picture of a god outside of you, but that is not the true God. And when someone comes and tells you who He really is, the idea is blasphemous. No one wants to believe that he is creating the conditions of his life; but God is the only causative power, as there is nothing but God. Everything is caused by Imagination. He is the only reality. So, how can you believe in him of whom you have never heard? And how can you hear of him unless there is a preacher? And how can there be a preacher unless he is sent? 522. Take my message to heart. The God spoken of in scripture is seated right here. He is in everyone as their wonderful human imagination. When you say, "I AM," that's God. If, right now you are assuming that you are other than what reason says you are and I ask you, "Who is imagining?" you would say, "I AM." At that very moment you have spoken God's name and all things are possible to God. So without the consent of anyone you can move from where you are to   where

you would like to be by a simple change of attitude. But your move must be fixed so that when you wake or sleep you remain in that attitude, for the state to which your thoughts constantly return constitutes your dwelling place, and your world is forever externalizing your dwelling place.

523.   Don't try to be holy. God isn't making good people, holy people.God is making creators, just like himself. If you think you are holy, that is not the key in to paradise. No matter how good you are, no matter how holy you think you are, holiness is not the key that allows you to enter that special grace, your creativity. God is doing it for you, working on you, bringing you to complete fruition and fulfillment. Try this principal of imagining, and if there is one thing I think man could do to aid . . as something within a shell could aid the bird . . the key is given to us in the Book of Job. He complained and complained of all the things that were happening to him, but his captivity was lifted when he prayed for his friends. If you would use your imagination lovingly on behalf of another and rejoice in his good fortune without any reward to you, you will see how this thing will begin to unfold within you.

524.   Your true environment is in your imagination! All that you behold,though it appears without, it is within, in your imagination . . of which this world of mortality is but a shadow. No matter what is taking place on the outside, it is but a symbol telling you what is taking place within; for the world is nothing more than yourself pushed out. Its image, alive in your imagination, overwhelms you.

525.   I wanted a trip I could not afford, yet I traveled over 5,000 miles bybeing still and saying to myself: "My awareness is God and all things are possible to him. therefore what I am imagining will come to pass." Then I began to imagine I was on a ship sailing towards Barbados. I remained faithful to that act, when suddenly . . after twelve years . . I received a letter from the family saying they would take care of all of my expenses if I would come home for Christmas. So I proved it. Then I tried it again and again, and the more I tried it the more I realized that the statement in the 46th Psalm was true: that God really is my own wonderful consciousness, for I learned to be still and know that I am God.

526.   In Genesis, the story is told of Isaac . . who was unable to see, butcapable of feeling . . calling to his son, Jacob, saying: "Come close my son that I may feel you. Your voice sounds like my son Jacob, but you feel like Esau." At that moment Jacob . . the imaginary, purely subjective state . . possessed the qualities of Esau, the objective world. So Isaac gave the imaginary state the right to be born. As Isaac, you can sit quietly and with your imaginary hands you can feel the difference between a tennis ball, a baseball, a football, and a golf ball. If they are nothing (because they are subjective and not objectively real to you at the moment) then you could not discriminate between them. But, if you can feel the difference between these so-called unrealities, then they must be real, although not yet made objective to your senses. The moment you give them reality in your mind's eye, they will become real in your world. Try it just for fun. Take an object and thank the being within you for the gift. Then thank the one on the outside, for within and without are vicarious, as is life; for by observing an odor, a look, or a feeling within, you will discover you are life itself.

527.   The law operates by faith. If you believe, no effort is necessary tosee the fulfillment of your every desire. If you go to the bank and have money deposited there equal to your check, you will give them your check in the belief that . . because of your faith . . they will give you the money you desire. Treat your desire in the same manner. Knowing your desire exists in your imagination, simply expect its fulfillment in your outer world. Try it. I have lived by this law all of my life and know, that by applying this principle, all of your desires will be fulfilled.

528.   So, in this world that profound story of the twins, Esau and Jacob, isnot understood because it does not make sense, but it is so very practical. The outer world may tell you that you can't have what you want, that you do not have the necessary education, experience, or means to achieve your goal. But your husband hates that outer you, and loving his bride (your human imagination), he gives you whatever you want.

529.   Now, the power of any imaginal act is in its implication. If he iscongratulating you on your good fortune, then you must have already received it, so accept his congratulation as a fact. Do that and you have subjectively appropriated your objective hope. Hoping that one day he   will

know of your good fortune and congratulate you, you have gone ahead in time, entered the state and allowed him to congratulate you. Now, go about your business and when you think of him, let him know (in your imagination) that he knows of your good fortune and that the day will come when it will be externalized. And when it does (and he will know of it) he will congratulate you on your good fortune on the outside, just as he did first on the inside.

530.	Imagination can see, touch, hear, taste and feel things other thanwhat your senses are experiencing right now. If you persist in acknowledging what your inner senses are telling you until you are persuaded of their reality, you will see their evidence. Then you will know from experience who Christ really is. Imagination is the only Christ Blake ever heard of. The apostles knew of no other, and any other belief was a false religion Blake called the devil. When you believe in someone on the outside, you have put him in conflict with the Second Commandment. You have made a graven image, yet [you were] told to "Make no graven image unto me." And when you think that someone other than yourself is Christ, your religion is false and you have a devil.

531.	If you attempt to change the world before you change your attitudetowards it, your struggle will be in vain. That which you dislike will change only to the degree that you change your attitude towards it. Until you do it cannot change, for the dislike is coming from within you. "Man is all Imagination, and God is Man and Exists in us and we in Him. The Eternal Body of Man is the Imagination and that is God himself." The secret of imagining is the greatest of all secrets, and everyone should try to unravel this mystery. Do you not realize that Jesus Christ is in you as your human imagination? Test yourself and see. You do not test another. Test yourself! See if what I tell you is true. I say your own wonderful human imagination is Jesus Christ, the life-giving spirit of all things. If this is true, you can test him who is your very self, and when you prove it you will know where, what, and who you really are. If I told a pillar of the Episcopal church (as the lady whose story I shared, was) that her imagination was Jesus Christ she would think me blasphemous.

When the lady came to me for help I did not call him Christ in her presence, but spoke of her imagination. She could use that and still have her little icons. She could assume her apartment in New York City was rented, but she could not believe that the being who made the mental transfer was Christ. Yet we are told that all things were made by him and without him was not anything made that is made. She mentally moved, and in less than twenty-four hours the move was physically accomplished. Now if all things are made by Christ and she knows exactly what she did, didn't she discover him? No, she didn't. She calls Christ her imagination, but separates her imagination from the Maker of worldly things.

Although she knows she brought about the rental of her apartment by her imaginal act, she still cannot bring herself to believe that her imaginal act was God in action. Raised to believe Jesus Christ was someone on the outside, she still worships a man based upon an artist's concept of him. But when you discover who Jesus Christ really is, you will know him as your very self. It does not yet appear what we should be, but we know that when he appears, we shall know him, for we shall be like him. "When scripture unfolds from within you, you will know that you and Christ are one."

532.   You are infinite love, but without the power of imagination, loveitself is eternal death. Start now to change your world to conform to your acts of love, but you cannot do it without imagination. Begin with self! Change your world and prove God's power is within you. Then you will know what it is to drink the cup which the Father has given you. It was God's infinite love that detached and allowed you to fall, for this separation is a fall and yet a beginning of a new creation. Just as the seed falls from man and a new creation begins, you fell and began a new creation, for God came with you as your human imagination.

533.   Now, the Bible teaches that permissible lies are allowed. Anassumption not based upon fact is a lie, is it not? We are told to emulate the story of the unjust steward who . . when told he might lose his job . . asked the one who owed one hundred measures of oil to give him fifty, another eighty, and still another sixty. And when he returned to his master the steward was commended for his wisdom. This steward falsified the record, the facts of life which memory claimed to be correct. Perhaps memory says you only have ten dollars in the bank, the rent is due, and there are no prospects of more money on its way. Or that your friend is ill or out of a job.

These are facts memory has recorded. You can falsify that record by a permissible lie, by seeing a thousand dollars in the bank and the rent as paid. By seeing one who is ill . . as well, or one who is unemployed . . as gainfully employed. That which appears so real is based on fiction anyway, and fiction is fact in the sense that it is all imagination! You can lift anyone out of the state into which he has fallen and place him in another, be it a state of want, illness, or failure. There are infinite states into which man may fall. If you will but believe that imagining creates reality, and there is no fiction, you can rewrite your life and give yourself and those within it beauty for ashes, gladness for mourning, and praise for faint-hearted. Believe in the reality of your unseen act, then watch it fulfill itself.

If you have proof that imagining creates reality, it will not matter what others think. All that matters is that you try it and allow imagination to prove himself in performance. I encourage you to live as fully and as graciously as you desire to, while you wait for God's Son to reveal himself in you. But don't think that because you do not live fully and well, you are better off in the eyes of your Father . . for you are not. He is only interested in the work He is doing in you; and when it is completed, you will be born from within, for until that happens you cannot enter the kingdom of God.

534.   Stop for a moment and see if you cannot relate the world roundabout you to an imaginal act. Then honor your imagination as God. Do not continue to simply acknowledge that your thoughts create your reality, but accept those thoughts for what they are, and that is God in action. And do not give your creative power over to a mortal man, believing he was the cause of your good fortune (or misfortune). Man is God's image . . the created, and not your imagination . . the Creator.

535.   Your Imagination knows all, is all, and is all powerful! If you shouldforget something, knowing that your own imagination is Jesus Christ, say: "Thank you Father that you always hear me." Do that and in the matter of moments the thought will return. Recognize your own wonderful human imagination as the only God, the only Lord Christ Jesus, for besides him there is no other. So the outstanding need this day is for a new Christology, a new knowledge of Christ, a completely new thinking of the human imagination. Until this is done unnumbered billions will be appropriated to fight poverty to

no avail. You can never give a poor man enough to satisfy him, and the day you stop giving he will cut your throat.

536.   The whole vast world is no more than man's imagining pushed out. Imust qualify that by saying that the world outside of man is dead, but Man is a living soul, and it responds to man, yet man is sound asleep and does not know it. The Lord God placed man in a profound sleep, and as he sleeps the world responds as in a dream, for Man does not know he is asleep, and then he moves from a state of sleep where he is only a living soul to an awakened state where he is a life-giving Spirit. And now he can himself create, for everything is responding to an activity in man which is Imagination. "The eternal body of man is all imagination; that is God himself." (Blake)

537.   Then wait in confidence for ways to open that you could not devise.No one knows how or when it will happen, but it will. You will find yourself walking across some bridge of incident that you did not consciously devise, which takes you to your freedom . . whatever that end may be. I tell you, "Man is all Imagination and God is Man and exists in us and we in Him. The Eternal Body of Man is the Imagination and that is God Himself." When this God awakes within you, His birth clothes you with everything said of Him in scripture. It is said that He is the light of the world; that He is love; that He is the power and the wisdom of the universe. May I tell you, when He awakes in you, you will be clothed with power, with wisdom, with light, and with love. And those whose eyes are opened into the inner, eternal world of thought will see you clothed as God.

538.   Leave the good and evil and eat of the Tree of Life. Nothing in theworld is untrue if you want it to be true. You are the truth of everything that you perceive. "I AM the truth, and the way, the life revealed." If I have physically nothing in my pocket, then in Imagination I have MUCH. But that is a lie based on fact, but truth is based on the intensity of my imagination and then I will create it in my world. Should I accept facts and use them as to what I should imagine? No. It is told us in the story of the fig tree. It did not bear for three years. One said, "Cut it down, and throw it away." But the keeper of the vineyard pleaded NO"! Who is the tree? I am the tree; you are the tree. We bear or we do not. But the Keeper said he would dig around the tree and feed it . . or manure it, as we would say today . . and see if it will not bear.

Well I do that here every week and try to get the tree . . you . . me to bear. You should bear whatever you desire. If you want to be happily married, you should be. The world is only response. If you want money, get it. Everything is a dream anyway. When you awake and know what you are creating and that you are creating it that is a different thing.

539.   Do not look to another as the cause of your misfortune. If you areperceiving a thing, it is penetrating your brain; therefore it exists in you. That which you are perceiving appears to exist in the surrounding world independent of your perception of it, but don't wait for it to change. If you desire a change in that which you are perceiving, you must produce the change in yourself. Ask no one to help you; simply persist in your new thoughts and let your changed thinking reproduce itself in your outside world, for it is only an out picturing of the world of thought within you. Try it. You can change your world as this prisoner did. In his imagination he moved in time to the day after his escape. You can do the same. Would your friends know of your success the day after it was achieved? Would they get together to discuss it? Make their gathering the scene from which you start. What would they say? Would some of them be jealous? Some happy for you? Put them all together and eavesdrop on their conversation. Then believe in what you have heard. Persist and your success is assured.

540.   In the Book of John, he tells an incredible story, saying: "I AM Godthe Father. When you see me, you see the Father. Do you not know that I AM in the Father and the Father in me?" Making one fantastic statement after the other, he adds: "I have told you before it takes place, so that when it does take place you will believe that I AM He." For we are told: "Unless you believe that I AM He, you die in your sins." John emphasizes over and over again that you must believe you are the one you would like to be, or you will never become it. Rather, you will remain what you believe yourself to be right now.

Your belief is always externalizing itself on the screen of space. It has to, for it is in you and not out there. When your belief becomes a fact and appears solidly real on the outside, it is because it is supported by you on the inside. The day you cease to believe in it, it will fade, for everything must be built on the foundation of belief. I believe I AM a success. I will remain a success only to the extent that I continue to believe I AM.

The day I stop believing, failure enters and success fades. You must believe you are in a certain state. You cannot forget it if you want to externalize that state. You may drop it after reaching a certain point, but if you want to keep it alive, you must do it within yourself; for nothing comes into being unsupported by an imaginal act, and nothing remains unless supported by that act. The day imaginal support is withdrawn the thing begins to vanish, and ceases to be in your world. This is true for a marriage, a friendship, or a business. If you know what you want, give it to yourself, for there is only one source of causation. That source is God (imagination). He is the dreamer in you who will awaken from this wonderful dream of life; and when he does, you will realize you have been dreaming all along. Many great poets have tried to tell this, but man cannot comprehend that the poet . . in touch with a deeper layer of his own being . . was awakened and recorded his experiences, until it happens in the individual.

541.   Isaiah tells you: "Your Maker is your husband; the Lord of hosts ishis name. He has called you like a wife forsaken and grieved in spirit, and will love you with everlasting love." In spite of everything you do, have done, or will do, God will forgive you . . for you are his emanation, his wife till the sleep of death is past. Regardless of the garment you wear, be it male or female, you are God's wife in this world. In symbolism however, God's wife appears in the form of a female. Blake tells us that He is God only, and She is God in you. As you journey you are God's emanation. But when the journey comes to its end you will know only God as your Maker, your husband, for you will inherit God. You will no longer be two, but you will become one being as you inherit yourself! Remember: you have only one lover, only one husband. He is your own wonderful Human Imagination, called God. It is he who gives you everything you fall in love with. But if you pray to a little statue made by human hands you are serving a false God. One day you will know that this world, which seems so real, is a dream.

542.   Although it doesn't seem possible, you and I were detached fromthat infinite field of beauty by an act of love. We were made subject unto futility, not by our own will but by the will of him who intended to give himself

to us. But in order to do it we had to be individualized by complete incarnation, complete insulation where we think we are human. Being a member of a family, having friends, and living in a world of people, you are insulated and completely separated. This incarnation is essential to your individuality, and when you begin to awake you awaken to the realization that you are he who subjected yourself, for you become the very being the world calls God the Father.

543.   Believe my words! Trust your imagination! Having reproducedhimself in you, all things now exist in your imagination. If you desire changes, produce them first on the inside. Penetrate that which exists in you, as that penetration will compel the outside to conform to the changes which you, the potter brought to pass. The only way to prove this is to try it. Imagine a scene which would take place after your desire has been fulfilled. Do not concern yourself as to how it is going to happen; simply go to the end. The most creative thing in you is your power to imagine a thing into existence. We are told in the Book of Hebrews that, "The things which are seen are made out of things which do not appear." No one can see your thoughts when you sit down to imagine. They are unseen by the outer world, but you know what you have done. Now, because imagination and faith are what creates and sustains your world, if you do not have faith in what you have imagined, it will not come to pass. It cannot, because imagination and faith are two sides of the same coin.

544.   Take me seriously. When you know what you want in life, constructa scene which would imply your desire is fulfilled. See it as clearly as possible. Feel its naturalness. Experiment until you know the scene and all it implies is real. Now, to the degree that you believe in its reality, your experiment will become your experience. Do not stop there. Keep on imagining and share your results with others. Tell them how to free themselves from this bondage to Caesar. When you know who you really are, you will not envy anyone. How could you, when you know you are God . . imagination, and they are only yourself pushed out? If tomorrow, something comes into your life that is not to your liking, do not accept it, for this fact blinds the I of imagination. Remove the blindness by asking yourself what you would like, in place of what seems to be. Enter into that thought. Revel in   it

as though it were not a fact. Persuade yourself that it is. Believe in its reality and it will become your experience.

545.   Everything is created by the human imagination. There is no otherGod. You can use your imagination wisely and create a heaven here on earth, or use it foolishly and create the world's havoc; but there is only one power, called the Lord God Jehovah in the Old Testament, and Jesus Christ in the New.

546.   Tonight ask yourself: "Who am I? Where am I?" If you do not likeyour answers, assume you are the person you would like to be, living where you would like to live. Persist in this assumption and . . although denied by your senses and reason . . if you persist your desires will harden into fact. Start now to take God's gift of his creative power and create! God detached and dropped you in love, for God is love. And when he did, he buried the gift of his creative power . . imagining . . called Jesus Christ . . in you. So now, like him, you can create, and as you do, your creation comes to life. Then you know that you no longer have to argue with the world, but can instantly change it to conform to the ideal that is in your being.

547.   Everyone should be completely consumed with the desire to knowhow a thing is made. I'll tell you how I make it. Knowing what I want, reason may tell me I can't get it and my senses may deny that I have it; but believing that my own wonderful human imagination is Christ and trusting myself, I assume I have it and drop it right there. I do not concern myself with what means will be employed for me to get it, I simply believe I already have it! I

believe that my own wonderful human imagination is Jesus Christ and all things are possible to him, even the recording of something that I have struggled all day to remember and cannot. Like Blake I turn to my human imagination, my divine body, for I know thee O Lord, when thou ariseth upon my eyes, even in this dungeon. So when I awake in the morning and imagination returns to make me alive, I trust it implicitly. Perhaps I can't remember something, but would like to, so I say: "Thank you Father, you always hear me." Then as I walk the earth memory appears out of the nowhere. Perhaps it is a poem, a saying, or an article I have misplaced; but when I turn to Him and in thankfulness request its memory, my Heavenly Father always gives it to me. This I know from experience.

548.   No matter what you are doing, can you see clearly what you want todo and carry on a conversation inwardly with a friend which will imply that which you desire is now a fact? Then do it. For on higher levels of Imagining inner activity is revealed by inner conversation. If man would listen to what he is inwardly saying, he would know what he is setting in motion. As man walks the street if he would pause and say "what am I saying now?" he would find that 99% are justifying failure. But we are told, "You are without excuse for you have seen him and his work, yet you deny it." When you hear the word God or Jesus Christ you think of some being external to your own imagining, but there is none for Imagining is God. That is what lights every being in the world, and as you imagine, so you will become. So no matter what your present limitations are, you can start now to dream the most noble dream, and you can walk through this door tonight as though it is true knowing that your Imagining is God. There is no fiction. You can write your own novel and realize it. Even someone in a dungeon may be imagining and who knows what he may call forth. If I were in a dungeon I would move the world if necessary to get out. A body may be physically confined, but you cannot confine God. Man only sees the proximate cause; the real cause of something you cannot see; for the invisible power is what is creating.

549.   Your assumption, though false in the sense that it is denied by yourreasonable mind, if persisted in will harden into fact. You do not need to know the means that will be employed to bring your assumption to pass; all you are required to do is persist in your assumption and allow your own wonderful human imagination to give it to you. All things are possible to your imagination. It's up to you to provide the necessary link between your assumption and its fulfillment. That link is faith. Having assumed your desire is fulfilled, your faith in that assumption will cause it to harden into fact. That is the law.

550.   Everyone here . . your invisible presence is God, but if you imaginemoney into being and you make a million, suddenly you worship the million, not the power that made it possible. You enter a certain social circle and then you forget that you brought it into being by imagining and now you

think this group is what is all-important. So man forgets and exchanges the glory of the immortal God for the image of a mortal man or something that vanishes. For everything visible will vanish; but you will not vanish. Even this great land will one day be washed by the sea but you will not be. That which brought things into being cannot cease to be.

551.   I say: everything is possible to anyone who knows who he is. Theaverage person does not know God, for if he did he would honor his imagination as God. Those who know God have discovered that when they imagine a state something happens and it takes form in their world.

552.   You can attain any goal if you believe that your own wonderfulhuman imagination is the Lord Jesus Christ. Imagine something, accept it in gratitude and watch it come to pass. May I tell you: you have always been doing it, but your memory is so short you do not recognize your own harvest. If your memory awoke you would see that everything happens because you at one time imagined it, (mostly in fear) and then dropped it. You planted the seeds of the tares and the wheat, the events and circumstances of your world, but have forgotten the planting. So I tell you: you are as free as you want to be if you will believe in Christ. He is not on the outside but in you, as your own wonderful human imagination!

553.   Forever justifying our world . . claiming he slapped me first, or shepushed me . . we speak with the voice of hell, the voice of self-justification. But in heaven it is all forgiveness of sin, because all things exist in heaven, the human imagination! Nothing happens on the outside that did not first take place in you, so you must forgive by changing the cause. If you try to justify or condemn, you live in the state of hell, for everything is taking place in you! Now seemingly separated from the Father, don't despair; for he was built in you from eternity.

554.   If you believe what the churches teach you may think that you arenot entitled to the good that you desire (read Romans 1:20) Ever since the creation of the world his invisible nature, namely, his eternal power and deity, has been clearly perceived in the things that have been made. So they are without excuse; for although they knew God, they did not honor him as God or give thanks to him, but they became futile in their thinking and their

senseless minds were darkened, claiming to be wise, they became fools, and exchanged the glory of the Immortal God for images resembling mortal man or birds or animals or reptiles . . . "and then they worshiped and served the creature rather than the Creator."

555. So I say to all: the one who makes everything is the humanimagination. This may seem cruel to one who is now experiencing pain, but it is true. I have suffered. I have known physical pain. Even though I may say I caught the flu, I know I caught it within me. I read the paper where I learned that 50 per cent of the people had the flu, and . . becoming a statistic . . I made it fifty-one. I have experienced its aches and pains, and learned a lesson. Now I know that even though I have experienced the drama of Jesus Christ, I am still subject to everything man is subject to. I know that I cannot point to any other cause other than my own imagination, as cause cannot come from the outside. If I am in pain, the cause is mine. We are told in Galatians that God . . your imagination . . is not mocked. That as you sow, so shall you reap.

556. You can prove you are all imagination if you believe it, for you liveby your beliefs. Lip service is not enough. Belief must become alive. Do you really believe your imagination makes all things? Then test yourself and see. When confronted with any problem, immediately construct an imaginal solution. Enter into that image and abide in its truth. Always remember who the maker is, for he makes things out of that which does not appear. He is like quicksilver, but you can test him best in a daydream. Fawcett said: "Divine imagining is like pure imagining in ourselves. It lives in the very depth of our soul underlining all of our faculties, including perception, but streams into our surface mind least disguised in the form of creative fantasy." All dreams proceed from God whether they be in the day, or night. Everything is preceded by a dream, called an imaginal act!

557. In the 64th chapter of the Book of Isaiah we read: "O Lord, thou artour Father; we are the clay. Thou art our potter; we are the work of thy hand." When you hear the words Lord, Father, and potter, do you think of another? I certainly hope not. The word "Lord" is Jod He Vau He [pron. "Yod Hey Vav Hey"] which is defined as "I AM". Your own wonderful I AMness is the

Lord, your Father. And the word "potter" means "imagination; that which is shaping your world." Imagination is the Lord, the potter, the shaper of your world, molding it into its present form.

558.   At the end of the drama it is said that one who knew Jesus betrayedhim. Now, in order to betray someone, you must know his secret! So the one who knows the secret betrays him. That one is self! God is self-revealed. Unless God reveals himself to you, how will you ever know him? Turning to those who did not know him, Jesus said: "Now that you have found me, do not let me go, but let all these go." Let every belief of a power on the outside go, but do not let the belief in your powerful imagination go . . for truth is within you. When you find the Maker in yourself, then no matter what arguments the priesthoods may give, do not believe them, for the Christ you seek is the human imagination. Tomorrow you may forget and be penetrated by rumors which disturb your body and cause you to suffer.

When this happens you must reestablish your harmony by imagining things are as you desire them to be. Living in this wonderful world, we cannot stop the penetration. To perceive another, that other must first penetrate your brain; therefore, he is within you as well as on the outside and independent of your perception. Cities, mountains, rivers and streams, must first penetrate your brain for you to be aware of them. At that moment of awareness they are within you, even though they still maintain a certain independence of your perception and are without. Treat this inner penetration seriously and you will discover all you need to do is adjust your thinking. That you are all imagination and must be wherever you think you are. If you want to contact a friend, simply adjust yourself to his community by making there . . here, and then . . now. Visit him in his home by penetrating it within yourself. Give him your message and see his eyes light up with the pleasure of your words.

559.   We are told that Daniel oriented himself at an open window, wherehe looked toward Jerusalem. And those in the Mohammedan world pray looking towards what they call Mecca. But because Christianity takes place within, scripture is speaking of the Jerusalem within, and not on the outside at all. When you pray you do not prostrate yourself on the ground and look towards some eastern point in space, but adjust yourself   mentally

into your fulfilled desire. Although this technique is simple, it takes practice to become its master. Your true direction is to the knowledge of what you want. Knowing your desire, point yourself directly in front of it by thinking from its fulfillment. Silence all thought and allow the doors of your mind to open. Then enter your desire. Stay with your imagination as your companion. Start by thinking of your imagination as something other than yourself, and eventually you will know you are what you formerly called your imagination. It is possible to amputate a hand, leg, or various parts of the body . . but imagination cannot be amputated, for it is your eternal Self!

560.   Your own wonderful human imagination is the being that I speak ofwhen I speak of God. When I say, "God became as we are, that we may be as He is," I am speaking of your imagination. And you cannot get away from your imagination. "And by Him all things were made, and without Him was not anything made that was made." That's your imagination. There isn't a thing in this world that you see now and call it a fact that wasn't first only imagined: the building; the clothes you wear; the chairs on which you are seated; this little mike; . . everything was first only imagined, and then executed.

Well, if all things were made by Him, and without Him was not anything made that was made, . . good, bad or indifferent, try to find some other maker than your own wonderful human imagination. Try to find it. You may say: "Edison did it" . . in his imagination; "Einstein did it" . . in his imagination. Show me one other instrument other than the human imagination that conceived anything in this world, and that is God. "If all things were made by Him, and without Him was not anything made that was made," then you conclude that He must be the human imagination. So, I tell you, your own wonderful human imagination is the God of Whom I speak! That is the Being that actually will awaken within you. But, now, to get things in this world, assume that you are. "All things are possible to Him."

Assume that you are the man that you want to be . . or the woman that you want to be. And, although at the moment of your assumption your reason and your senses deny it, if you dare to persist in that assumption as though it were true, that assumption . . in a way unknown to your rational, conscious mind . . will harden into fact. It knows how to actually build that series of events necessary to make it so in your world. If you really want to be what you call "secure", . . say, in finances, dare to assume that you are secure, and live as though you were; sleep as though you were; and then it will happen in your world that will cause you to leave your present environment and move on into the state that you have assumed. If you wait for things to change before you dare to assume, you will wait forever. Circumstances cannot change of themselves. You change them by changing your concept of Self. To attempt to change the world before you change your own imaginal activity is to struggle against the very nature of things.

Now, you say: "Well, I am reaping these things in my world, and I didn't make them." No, . . you have forgotten the blossom time. What you are now reaping is simply the fruit of some forgotten blossom time. You have a very faulty memory. We all have. We can't remember when we set in motion what we are now reaping as a harvest; but everything in our world was once planted as an imaginal act, and it has not a physical cause, . . it has an imaginal cause. Every natural effect in this world has an imaginal cause, and not a natural cause. A natural cause only seems; it is the delusion of a faulty memory, because man cannot remember the blossom time when he actually set it in motion.

561. Everything, that can be seen, touched, explained, argued over, is to the imaginative man nothing more than a means, for he functions, by reason of his controlled imagination, in the deep of himself where every idea exists in itself and not in relation to something else. In him there is no need for the restraints of reason. For the only restraint he can obey is the mysterious instinct that teaches him to eliminate all moods other than the mood of the fulfilled desire.

562.   That is what I mean by imagining creating reality, for an assumptionis faith; and without faith it is impossible to please your own wonderful human imagination. Divine Imagination, containing all, reproduces itself in human imagination; therefore, the human imagination contains all. The world is the human imagination pushed out. Not knowing this, man cheats himself, murders himself, declares war against himself, and does all sorts of evil against himself; but do not let yourself be intimidated by the

horror of the world. Leave it alone, for it is only the misuse of the power exercised by sleeping mankind.

563.	Now, you have friends. They know your present position and theconditions that surround you. If they are not as you would like them to be, let your friends know . . not verbally or outwardly . . but in your imagination. See them seeing you as they would have to see you, the day after they know things are just as you want them to be.

564.	"The secret of imagining is the greatest of all problems, to thesolution of which every man should aspire; for supreme power, supreme wisdom, and supreme delight, lie in the solution of this great mystery." Imagination is the Jesus Christ of scripture, and when you solve the great mystery of imagining, you will have found the cause of the phenomena of life. Imagination is called "Jehovah" in the Old Testament and "Jesus" in the New, but they are one and the same being. Divine Imagination, containing all, reproduces itself in the human imagination; therefore, all things exist in the human imagination. When you solve the problem of imagining, you will have found Jesus Christ, the secret of causation.

565.	Eventually we are all going to know we are the Father; but in themeanwhile, persistence is the key to a change in life . . more income, greater recognition, or whatever the desire may be. If your desire is not fulfilled today, tomorrow, next week or next month . . persist, for persistency will pay off. All of your prayers will be answered if you will not give up. My old friend, Abdullah, gave me this exercise. Every day I would sit in my living room where I could not see the telephone in the hall. With my eyes closed, I would assume I was in the chair by the phone. Then I would feel myself back in the living room. This I did over and over again, as I discovered the feeling of changing motion. This exercise was very helpful to me. If you try it, you will discover you become very loose with this exercise. Practice the art of motion, and one day you will discover that by the very act of imagining, you are detached from your physical body and placed exactly where you are imagining yourself to be . . so much so that you are seen by those who are there.

Being all imagination, you must be wherever you are in imagination. Moving in your imagination, you are preparing a place for your desires to be fulfilled. Then you return, to walk through a series of events which will lead you up to where you have placed yourself. In imagination, I can put myself where I desire to be. I move and view the world from there. Then I return here, confident that . . in a way unknown to me . . this being who can do all things and knows all things, will lead me physically across a bridge of incident up to where I have placed myself. You can move in imagination to any place and any time. Dwell there as though it were true, and you will have learned the secret of prayer.

566.   Everyone here, you can be what you want to be, no matter what yourdream is, if you are willing to let God do it, God being your own Imagining. You walk completely suspended above appearances and you will become what you desire. This is the only Christianity I know . . the freedom to exercise this divine art of Imagining. Now you try it. If you are here for the first time I challenge you to disprove it. Everyone has the same power. Because one has a million does not make him any more a creator than you are. Be careful what you are imagining for what you are Imagining you will create, though it may convulse the world. I hope you have the Revised Version of the Bible for it is from what I have quoted tonight. It is more accurate in meaning if not as orally beautiful as the King James Version.

567.   In my Father's house are unnumbered mansions. Unnumbered statesof consciousness. If it were not so, would I have told you that I go to prepare a place for you? And when I go I will come again and receive you to myself, that where I am you may be also. In this statement Imagination is telling you he is the Father for "No one comes to the Father but by me." Only when you come to the awareness that your human imagination is the phenomenon, the source of all life, will you find the Father.

568.   So tonight, you take me seriously; and when you go home . . or startit here, . . you put into practice this greatest of all secrets; the secret of imaging. There is no greater secret in the world. Every child born of woman is alive because it was imagined. And imaging is God in action. That's the soul of man . . imaging; and that is the power of God. And the power of God is Christ. And that is the wisdom of God, and the wisdom of God is Christ. A child   can

imagine. Well, that's Christ. That is Christ crucified on that little tiny garment, and it suffers with everything that that little child imagines, or it enjoys with everything the little child imagines. It wears all the stripes and all the blows that man in his misuse of that power will do. He doesn't criticize him. He waits upon me as indifferently . . and as quickly . . when the will in me is evil as when it is good. That way, He bears all my stripes. He bears all of my misuse of His power, knowing that in the end, I will awaken and use it only lovingly.

569.   Having been taught God was another, I had formed a mental conceptof him that comforted me and allowed me to pray to someone other than myself. But when I found him, I found him in myself, as myself! Then I

knew I could not pray to another; I must turn within and appropriate, for everything is contained within my own wonderful human imagination!

570.   No matter what it is you desire, remember: nothing is impossible.What is now proved was once only imagined, so begin by imagining a state and persuading yourself that you are in it. Blake said: "The ancients believed that if you are self-persuaded, it was so. There was a time in Imagination when a firm persuasion removed mountains." You can remove the seemingly mountainous obstacles which confront you by simply ignoring them and assuming the end. And if you have to go over the mountain, you will, or the mountain will be removed. Whatever is necessary to be removed for you to fulfill what you have assumed, will be done for you as long as you remain faithful to yourself, the source of all life.

571.   Browning began his wonderful poem, "Easter Day" with the words: "How hard it is to be a Christian." And Chapman said: "Christianity has not been tried and proved wanting. It has been tried and found difficult and therefore given up." Why? Because a Christian cannot pass the buck and blame another. Christianity is built upon the foundation that all are one. That man is forever drawing conformation of what he is doing within himself. That your world bears witness to what you are doing to yourself. This is difficult to accept, yet it is Christianity. No man comes unto me, save my Father . . imagination . . who sent me calls him. I and my Father are one, therefore I call all those who enter my life to reveal to me what I am doing in my imagination.

572.	Now, in order to prove that the law works, you must try it. Have agoal. Your goal may be peace of mind, health or marriage. You name it. Knowing your own wonderful human imagination is the one and only cause of your life, conceive a scene which, if true, would imply the fulfillment of your goal. Do not allow yourself to observe the action, but put yourself in the center of the scene and allow your friends to congratulate you on your good fortune. Accept their congratulations without embarrassment. Enter into the spirit of the scene and remain there until it feels real, then drop it in confidence that the imaginal act was performed by God. How do I know this? Because God's name forever and ever is I AM. If at the time of your imagining I had asked you what you were doing, you would have said: "I am imagining." At that moment you called forth your desire with His name. Every time you imagine, God is acting and all things are possible to him. All you need to do now is wait patiently, confident that your desire will externalize itself, and when it does you have found the cause of creation. Then tell your sleeping brothers, who wait patiently for their world to change while they activate its continuance. Nothing happens on the outside! Everything has to be initiated on the inside first. Read the morning paper, turn on the television or radio, and react to what you hear and see, and that reaction is an imaginal act which will cause unlovely experiences to people your world. As you reap your harvest, you may not relate your present experience to what you did, but you had to have done it or you couldn't be aware of it now, for everything is yourself pushed out, for you and God are one.

573.	You must forget the concept of Jesus Christ as a little man externalto yourself, for it is Christ in you who is your hope of glory. All things are made by him, whether they be good or ill, lovely or unlovely. An artist doesn't have to create only the beautiful, but can create anything, and so it is with God. You can find him by testing your wonderful human imagination. I have searched for and found Jesus Christ to be my own wonderful human imagination. I now know that everything in my world was first imagined by me. I may not always remember the imaginal act relative to the unlovely things I have experienced, but I have imagined and watched its fulfillment in my world. I know that although I may not remember the imaginal act, I must have committed it, for I cannot reap that which I have not sown.

574.   I urge you to set your hope fully on the grace that is coming to youat the unfolding of Jesus Christ in you. Use the law towards beautifying your world and getting all of the lovely things you feel you need. Don't ask anyone's permission; simply appropriate it in your own wonderful human imagination. Imagine and live by imagining, . . morning, noon, and night. It will not fail you, but remember: you are the operant power. Knowing what to do is one thing. Doing it is another; and we are called upon to be doers of the word and not just hearers only, deceiving ourselves. You can read one of my books over and over again. You can tell others what the book says, but if you never apply its message, the mere reading of its words will not benefit you. But if you will test your imagination, it will prove itself in performance.

575.   All cause is spiritual! Although a natural cause seems to be, it is adelusion of the vanishing vegetable memory. Unable to remember the moment a state was imagined, when it takes form and is seen by the outer eye its harvest is not recognized, and therefore denied. "There is a moment in each day that Satan cannot find, nor can his watch fiends find it, but the industrious find this moment and it multiplies. And when it once is found, it renovates every moment of the day if rightly placed." (William Blake) The word Satan means doubt. Desiring a certain state, reason may tell you it will be difficult to attain, and your friends may say it is impossible. If you listen to them and doubt your desire's fulfillment, Satan has made himself known to you. Your protractors . . God and Satan . . are always with you, for one is faith and the other doubt. Can you imagine you are the one you would like to be, and remain faithful to that assumption? If you can and do, it will appear, and you will realize that its spiritual cause was the moment of assumption.

576.   No one would ever agree with another as to what is right and what iswrong, for we all have different values. What is right to one is wrong to another. We came down into the world of death because we ate of the tree of knowledge of good and evil, and we are told that the only thing that displeases God is the eating of that tree, and unbelief. If you think another is the cause of your misfortune, you are sinning and missing your mark in life. There is only one cause for all of the phenomena of your life, and that is God, whose eternal name is I AM. When you really believe this, you will not deny the harvest you are reaping. It may be unpleasant, but you will know that it couldn't happen unless you sowed it, so accept your harvest and then   plant something lovely in its place. Never deny that one and only cause, which is your own wonderful human imagination!

577.   If you confine yourself to the human belief of truth, you will bestuck in that groove; for every moment of time you are confronted with the facts of life. Knowing your social, intellectual, and financial background, you could not get out of the environment in which you were placed. My family did not accept these so-called facts of life. They climbed out of poverty by using their imagination. Knowing what they wanted, they imagined their desire was an external fact. They remained faithful to this imagined state, and in time they became what they imagined themselves to be. That is the law.

578.   In the parable of Isaac and his two sons, Esau and Jacob, Isaac isblind. Desiring to be felt as his brother Esau was, Jacob clothed himself with the skins of a goat. Clothed so that his blind father could feel him through the sense of touch, Jacob deceived his father into giving him his blessing. Let us extract the psychological meaning from this story. Reason says you are not the man you want to be. Closing your eyes to the obvious facts of life, you deny everything reason dictates by mentally clothing yourself in your desired state. Let people see you there. Imagine until you are actually standing where you want to stand. Actually doing the things you would do if your desire was now an obvious fact. Do this, and you are clothing yourself in the outer garment of naturalness.

When you open your eyes to the facts of life, they will deny everything you have done . . but you know what you did. You caught a precious moment which doubt cannot find, or his help-mates find. You have become one of the industrious, for you found the moment and clothed yourself with the feeling of fulfilled desire and . . like Isaac . . you have given your blessing to the moment and cannot take it back. Isaac would not retract his blessing; so when Esau (the reasonable, rational mind) returned, its right to live had been taken away by Jacob (the smooth-skinned desire). Jacob was rightly named, for the word means "the supplanter." Isaac explained to Esau that, even though Jacob deceived him, the moment could not be called back. It was on its way toward fulfillment. And when it appears, its suddenness is only the emergence of a hidden continuity.

579.   I urge you not to despair. If you have tried and tried to imagine, yetfailed, don't give up, try to be more intense. Try to be more believing concerning the reality of your imaginal act. Man, believing in the mechanism of the universe, finds it difficult to see it as imaginal, but it is. Tell the story of the Kennedys to the average man and he will say: so what? He cannot see that story as confirmation of the fact that imagining creates reality. You could tell him a hundred such stories, but . . steeped in believing that this world is mechanical and must be moved on the outside . . man finds it difficult to understand that the world will reshuffle itself to reflect any change that takes place in the individual. But the change takes place in the imagination, not in the world!

580.   In the 2nd chapter of the Book of Jeremiah, the Lord said: "I plantedyou a pure seed, O Israel. How did you become degenerate?" I will tell you how! By going after foreign gods; by worshipping the gods of astrology, numerology, wealth, or so-called important people. By believing in things on the outside and seeing other causes for the phenomena of your life and not the only cause, who is God, your own wonderful human imagination, whose name is I AM! One day you will awaken to discover that you are the one and only God. But you aren't going to rob anyone, for it takes all your brothers, together, to form the one pyramid, and when this is accomplished the top stone will be put in place.

581.   God is the only source and there is no other. In the 87th Psalm it issaid that when this one is born, the Lord registers his people, and the singers and dancers alike say: "You are my springs." There is no other spring! No other cause! No other source! Whether you are dancing or singing here, you are asleep and your own wonderful human imagination is causing your life to be what it is. Do not blame another for the events in your life. There is no one you can turn to as its cause, and don't let anyone blame you, as they are creating their own world by what they are imagining. If one imagines unlovely things for another, they are going to produce them . . not in the other, but in themselves.

582.   This world is made up of infinite states which you may clotheyourself with. If you do not like the state you are in, you can get out of it by taking a heavenly moment and assuming you have moved. You can put

yourself into any state, be it wealth or poverty. If you don't enjoy poverty, don't get into the state. I have no desire for fabulous wealth. I do not want the responsibility connected with it. I can't see how anyone who is fabulously wealthy has any time for spiritual awareness. Morning, noon, and night he must watch his portfolio. The first thing he does in the morning is read the financial section of the newspaper. He reads it as some ladies read the social section . . as though it really matters. There are those who read the obituaries first and make their living from it. My father-in-law was a very prominent man in New York City when he died.

Shortly after his death, his wife received hundreds of letters from people claiming he had ordered something from them and had promised to pay, and many of the writers had misspelled his name! Her lawyer told her to forget the letters, as many people made their living that way. You can't conceive of anything that someone is not already doing. Everything is possible because imagining creates reality. And don't think you can imagine quietly, because your world is a record of your imaginal acts. Nothing appears by accident. You may not remember the moment you imagined it, so you cannot relate your spiritual cause to its natural effect; but every natural effect has a spiritual cause. All causes are spiritual, all imaginal, for "Man is all imagination and God is man and exists in us and we in him. The eternal Body of man is the imagination and that is God Himself." (William Blake)

583.   I have told you the story of how Moses did not cross into thepromised land, but Joshua did. You may not be familiar with scripture, but Joshua's original name was Hoshea (Numbers 13:16) The word "Hoshea" means "savior or salvation." Put the prefix "Je" before Hoshea and the meaning changes to "he by whom Jehovah is saved." Moses represents the pattern man, and Hoshea . . creative power. When that power is fertilized, Joshua . . the pattern . . unfolds, and the individual occupying the state enters the promised land. What you saw in the beginning was the perfect egg, but it was not fertilized. A sperm must penetrate the surface of an egg in order to fertilize it; yet no hole appears in this perfect egg either before or after penetration, because it is all imagination. Being all imagination, you do not need to go through any door to put yourself into a closed room, or break down any wall when you depart. Having entered without the use of a hole, you can depart without leaving any breakage relative to your entrance or

departure. So it is with a little sperm. It penetrates the surface of an egg and it leaves no hole either before or after penetration; but unless it penetrates, that egg remains just a perfect pattern of what could be. It takes the sperm to penetrate and make it alive. I urge you to test your creative power on this level.

Take every moment you can and clothe yourself in the feeling that your wish is fulfilled. Feel its reality and do not forget that moment, for it is productive. In its own good time, that moment will appear in this world, properly clothed as an objective fact. No matter who it takes to aid the birth of your imaginal act, he will appear. If it takes an army to bring it to pass, an army of men will do it. You do not have to determine the way, all you need do is imagine. Just as you would plant a seed in the ground, confident that it will grow, so you can drop your fulfilled desire into your mind, confident that it will appear as an objective fact. If you want to be a man of wealth, assume that you are.

You see: the man of wealth and the poor man are the same being. The individual who occupies the poor state is God's emanation who has fallen into the state of poverty. He does not differ, however, from the individual who occupies the state of wealth. The man in the state of wealth may have lots of money, but he is the same being, in a spiritual sense, as the man who is poor. The only difference is that the poor man does not know he can leave the state of poverty.

584.   When you know what you want, use your sense of feeling. Let thefeeling of satisfaction so fill your being that the idea ceases to be a desire, but has evoked motor elements. These awaken sensory sensations within you causing the desire's fulfillment. Imagination is nothing more than sensory states. Learn to go beyond an idea by feeling its reality. Then turn to another and still another, as the being who is feeling it begins to awaken within you. Fulfill all of your desires while you are here, and then when you least expect it, the Divine Breath will breathe upon that immortal tomb where you are buried. And you will awaken to find yourself completely sealed in your Holy Sepulcher where you have been dreaming your life into being. This world is made up of horrible dreams which the one within every individual is dreaming. That one must and will awaken, as you hear the story and put it

into practice through repentance. The word "repentance" comes from the Greek word "metanoia," which means "a radical change of attitude." This change must be so radical that it gets right down to the root, the I AM! Think of your world as your mirror. Do you like what you see there? You know you can live with it or ignore it, but perhaps you would like to see it differently. If you would, repent by persuading yourself that you are seeing a world to your liking. Persist in your repentance, for to the degree that you are selfpersuaded it is so, it will be so.

585.   Let the world turn their back upon this law. That is perfectly allright, but you go your way using your talent. And when you least expect it, all that is said in scripture concerning Jesus Christ will be yours to experience in the first person, singular, present tense. Then you will know beyond all doubt who Jesus Christ really is. When you know who you are, it will not matter what the world says. Let the billion Christians and the two billion nonChristians go their way. If they want to question or ridicule you, turn your back and walk away. Having found the real Christ, imagination, you have found the great secret to the mystery of all life.

586.   Scripture speaks of the stone, the water, and the wine. The stone isthe literal story, the allegory. When man discovers the fictitious nature and character of the story by turning within, he has struck the rock and . . like Moses . . water flows from it. The first miracle, or sign, is recorded in the Book of John, as turning water into wine. The story comes first. That's the stone. If you accept the story as literally true, you have accepted the stone. When you discover the fictitious character and extract the true meaning of the story, you have found the psychological water. A dog is the symbol of faith.

Her faith is now in the psychological meaning of these great truths, and as she applies them she will convert them into wine. Believing that imagining creates reality, dare to imagine you are now what you would like to be. Do that and you are turning the water into wine. We are told that when Jacob brought his flock into the field, the well was covered with a stone. He rolled it away, watered his flock and replaced the stone. Jacob did not turn the water into wine, but removed the stone which covered the tomb of water. This is an allegory. You must use your imagination to extract the water (meaning) and feed your flock. Every scriptural story has a psychological meaning. Find the meaning and you are extracting water from stone.

587.   Can you imagine what it would be like if you were the man (thewoman) you would like to be? Sustain that imaginal act as though it were true, and no power in the world can stop it from becoming true, because there is no other power. Try it beginning tonight. Take a glorious concept of life. Nothing less than the very best, and simply imagine it to be true about you and those you love. Start with your immediate circle and . . although at the moment your circle may deny it by reason of what they are doing . . persist in your assumption as though it were true, and it will harden into fact. Grant all of your sleeping brothers their right to pursue God in some other direction. They will never find him in any other way, save by experiencing the story of Jesus Christ. Then and only then will they know the true knowledge of God.

588.   "Father, forgive them for they know not what they are doing." If youknow that you are the cause of your sorrow, can you not forgive the one who submitted it? Must you condemn a shadow, when you are its cause? Everyone who comes into your world is drawn there by your Father, with whom you are one. If he who enters insults or offends you and you know you are the cause of his seeming offense, can you not forgive him? Can you not say: "Father, forgive him for he knows not what he is doing?" Your world is filled with those who are under compulsion to play their part because of what you have imagined. You may have forgotten your imaginal acts, and may even deny you ever entertained such thoughts; but they could not come if you had not called them out of yourself; therefore, you must forgive them, for they only did what you asked them to do.

589.   But I tell you, every child born of woman has the greatest talent ofthem all . . the human imagination. A man sentenced for life could be in a dungeon imagining himself elsewhere, and if it takes an earthquake to set him free, an earthquake will appear. But if he sits in the dungeon believing the world is against him, he will remain there. But, while there in his body, he can walk the streets as a free man by using his talent. He can view the world from a free state and in a way that no one knows, he will be set free. Whatever your desire may be, is possible and can be yours if you will imagine its possession and dwell in its fulfillment.

But I warn you: Do not imagine with hate in your heart, because you are only hurting yourself. Although you may not realize it, the world is yourself pushed out. It is forever bearing witness to you who are all Imagination.

Make no attempt to change the world until you first change your attitude towards it. Change your thinking and the world will reshuffle itself to reflect your new thoughts. This is the talent of which the gospels speak. To one five talents were given. To another, two and another, one. Then came the day of accounting and all those who had expanded their talents were invited to enter into the joy of their master. And those who were afraid to test their Imagination, who wouldn't even try it, were condemned, and the knowledge of the power that they are was taken from them.

The talent is God's gift to you. It is entrusted to you for your use. Use your talent tonight by sleeping in the assumption that you are now .. not tomorrow .. but now, the person you would like to be. In the morning, persist in your assumption by allowing the world to see you as they would have to see you, were you now the one you would like to be. Although your reason and senses deny your assumption, if you persist your desire will harden into fact.

590.   Imagination truly creates out of nothing! Thoughts call forth a thingthat is not seen, as though it were happening. This is accomplished by an imaginal concept touched by feeling. Hearing of the success of another and feeling their joy builds a structure which will project itself on the screen of space. Calling the projection reality, one may think it was created from the outside. But what happened had to happen as it did, for there are no accidents.

591.   When you have found the cause of the phenomena of your life, letevery other belief go. Should people urge you to eat certain food or observe certain days do not believe them, for there is nothing you can do on the outside that will ever commend you to God. You are defiled or purified by what comes out of your heart, not by what you eat or observe on the outside. Are you imagining good or evil for yourself, for the true vine is your own wonderful human imagination, and the world without is nothing more than your branches.

592.   Jesus Christ is God himself, who became you, individually. Yourawareness is He. When you imagine, God is acting. He is the true vine and the vinedresser, for he is your imagination, imagining you. If you really understand this, you will start pruning your thoughts. If you don't and continue to believe Jesus Christ is other than your Self, you will persist in allowing your wanton energy to run wild, to swell into irregular twigs, and bear unlovely things in your world. When you become aware of those in need, even though you do not know them personally, do you use your imagination to lift them from that state? That is what you are called upon to do. If you represent them to yourself as you would like them to be, and persuade yourself it is true, that branch will change in your world. You do not eliminate the state of need. It remains for anyone to be aware of, but you . . having lifted yourself out of the state . . see it no more. Prune your vine morning, noon, and night; and then . . when you least expect it . . a series of wonderful, supernatural experiences will be yours, as God reveals himself in you . . not as another, but as your very Self. Then you will say, from personal experience, "I AM He."

593.   Do not be concerned with the horrors of the world; simply rememberthat all is ordered and correct. Instead, fall in love with the I AM within you and change your world. God made it as it is now and he can change it, for your husband is a creator. Everything in your world can be traced back to your own wonderful human imagination, who is God. Fall in love with the state you now desire to occupy and to the degree that you are self-persuaded, you will enter it. Don't believe in anyone outside of your own wonderful human imagination! Every coin is inscribed with the statement: "In God we trust" yet I wonder how many trust in God . . and not the coin! If you really believe in God, you can be penniless, yet walk in the assumption of wealth and be wealthy. Learn to trust your own wonderful human imagination, for he is the only God. Do that and you will never go wrong!

594.   The entire 15th chapter of the Book of John is devoted to thispruning of the vine. He starts off: "I AM the true vine. My Father is the vinedresser. Every branch of mine that bears no fruit he prunes, that it may bear more fruit." The tree in your garden may be lovely to look at and it may pain you to cut a certain branch, but you know you must do it if you want good fruit next year. That is life. Consciousness (the I AM) is the eternal vine.

Your eternal body is the Imagination, which is God himself. We are all members of the divine body . . Jesus; therefore humanity is truly the body of the Lord Jesus Christ. Every child is part of that universal body; and when he knows that Jesus Christ is his own wonderful human imagination, he is confused for the moment, until the realization rearranges itself within him. Then he takes himself in hand, determined to do something about it. I tell you from experience, if you will take yourself in hand and really believe in Christ in you to the point that you will turn to no other causation, but will prune your thoughts morning, noon, and night, your world will change. It will mold itself in harmony with the change which has taken place in you, for your outer world is forever reflecting your inner, imaginal acts.

595.   One must see the whole vast world as a psychological drama. Youmay think you have never committed adultery, but the moment you lust after anything, the stage is set by your imaginal act. Restraining the impulse is not good enough. The moment you have the impulse to steal, the act is committed. The impulse to hurt is the act of hurting. You may be afraid to carry out any act, but when the impulse appears, the act is committed. Once you understand this, you will forgive all, for there is only one son (who you are), doing your Father's will.

596.   You can write your own essay on success if that is your desire, andto the degree that you are self-persuaded it is true, you will give it life in your world. The secret is to imagine to the point of self-persuasion. Can you believe what you are imagining? There are not two of you . . you and Imagination! You are not reshaping a piece of pottery when you imagine, but yourself! You are moving into your desire. If you persist until you see exactly what you want to see, fix your position with the glue of feeling and remain there . . it will be reflected on the screen of space, just as your world is now reflecting the fixed state from which you are viewing it.

There are two worlds: the outer world of effect and the inner world of causation. That inner world, in the depth of your soul, is where the true drama of life goes on. It is there that God is endowing you with life-giving power. Now a living soul, you are being transformed into a life-giving spirit! On that day you will see this world from above, to discover it is dead and you are its animating power. Blake said: "Where man is not, nature is barren." This is true, for nature cannot produce anything by itself. Man, a living soul, causes things to appear alive by his animating power. Although you are now animating all that you behold, you are destined to become a life-giving spirit . . to fashion things in your own image, bring them forth, and endow them with the power to create life. Believe me, there is no fiction! Every thought you think will come to pass. You may think it is just a thought and will never become real, but it will.

597.   Born in the little island of Barbados, we kept ducks and chickens forour own consumption. If mother wanted a pair of ducks for a Sunday dinner, ten days prior she would tell one of her nine sons to put a brace of ducks aside. Now, our ducks were raised in the yard and fed on fish, which was cheap and plentiful . . and not on corn, which had to be imported and was very expensive. We could buy a bucket of fish scraps for a penny, so we fed the chickens and ducks fish; consequently they smelled of and tasted like fish. But if they were separated ten days or two weeks before you wanted them for dinner, and stuffed with corn and food of that nature, the entire texture of their flesh changed.

During that interval of time however, they could not be given even a little bit of fish. They had to have a complete, radical change of diet. If mother's command was not remembered until perhaps four days before the meal everyone knew it, because when the birds were plucked and the heat began to express the birds, the entire neighborhood knew the Goddard's were having fish for dinner, and no one could eat them. But if their diet was changed from fish to corn . . and only corn for that interval of time . . we had delicious ducks for dinner which tasted like ducks! Now, although we are not ducks we do feed on ideas. Feed your mind a certain idea for one week and you will change its structure. Continue for two weeks and you will be well fed on lovely thoughts.

You see, this is a fictitious world and you are its author. Nothing is impossible! It's all fiction anyway, so live nobly and dream beautiful dreams; for you are all imagination, and your human imagination is the Lord God, Jesus . . the Christ.

598.   There is no sin against the Holy Ghost other than man's belief thatsomething is impossible to his own wonderful human imagination! I want you to go all out! To put no limit on God's creative power. To imagine that which is unimaginable and to walk on the water, through faith. Water symbolizes your acceptance of life as psychological, and its drama as taking place in the Imagination. When you cease excusing yourself or anyone for life's experiences, and begin to rearrange the structure of your mind to feel your desire is fulfilled, you are walking on the water. Scripture speaks of the stone, the water, and the wind. Accept the facts of life and you are stepping down on stone. Change the facts in your imagination, and you have turned them into psychological truth, which then becomes a spiritual experience. When you live by this principle, you are walking on water, towards your birth from beyond.

599.   A friend recently shared a wonderful experience with me. It seems aneighbor was forever dropping in on her, constantly telling horrible stories about her friends. She tried to tell the woman how to change things by using her imagination, but she would not listen. And although she imagined her as a fine, positive, happy person, she remained in her negative state. Realizing the lady was a character my friend had to overcome, she began to change her thoughts. In her imagination she told the neighbor that she loved her. This she persisted in doing, until one day she realized she really did. That night she had this dream. She found herself sitting in the shade of a beautiful tree. A figure approached, looking like a goddess, in a long white gown with loose sleeves and a silver belt.

Suddenly she realized it was her friend, who came to say goodbye. They embraced and she felt a surge of love for that woman like she had never known for anyone before. The next day this lady came to her door and said: "I gave my notice this morning and have come to say goodbye." Then my friend added this thought: "If I could fall as much in love with the being within me as I did with this lady, I would be completely transformed . . which in turn, would produce great changes in my outer world of effects, for now I know my friend's transformation took place within me."

600.   The true vine is your own wonderful human imagination. When youbelieve this you will no longer imagine as you formerly did, but will prune

your thoughts every minute of every day. You will break the habit of feeling remorseful, depressed, or regretful. You will no longer think unkindly about another, because you will know that he is actually yourself pushed out, and appeared in your world because the Father in you called him. No one can come unto me unless I, who am one with the Father, call him. Even though he brings poison he does it because I gave it to him to bring. This is the story that is reenacted today, but not understood.

601.   Blake asked the question: "Why is it that the Bible is moreentertaining and instructive than any other book? Is it not because it is addressed to the Imagination, which is spiritual sensation, and only immediately to the understanding, or reason?" The one book, called the Bible, is composed of sixty-six books. Take this challenge. Read each book as though the depth of your soul is speaking to your surface mind. As though the ineffable Imagination is speaking to the human Imagination, and not to your immediate understanding or reasoning mind. Let us examine this thought. In his 2nd letter to the Corinthians Paul says: "We walk by faith and not by sight." When we walk by sight, we know our way by objects that the eye sees.

But Paul tells us to order our life by objects seen only in the imagination. In other words, when you know where you want to go and what you want to be, you are told not to rearrange your physical structure, but to walk by faith, viewing only the rearranged structure of your mind. And if you will remain faithful to that state of consciousness, what is seen only in your imagination will objectify itself in your world.

602.   Every event in life contains within itself something beyond itsphysical experience. Flowers symbolize the growth of plantings. During winter, when nothing grows, he planted seeds, which he will harvest not only in the world of Caesar, but also in the world of the Spirit, as we all do. I urge you now to use your imagination and walk on the water. Plant the seeds of desire in the depth of your soul and allow them to flower on earth. If you do not see their harvest immediately, believe what you did, for it will come whether you recognize it or not. And do not sin against the Holy Ghost by saying something is impossible, for God is your own wonderful human imagination and nothing is impossible to imagine.

603.   As the operant power of your imagination, you can tell where youare going and what you are doing by watching your thoughts. If certain events in your past are unlovely and you remember them, you are ordering their experience. But if you turn your back on the past by forgetting what lies behind and stretch forward to what lies ahead, you will order your conversations aright and become what you behold. This truth will never   be

disproved, but you are its operant power and must live by it. You need nothing on the outside, but can start just where you are; but you must walk in the direction you set up in your imagination.

Ask yourself this simple question: What would it be like if it were true that I am now the person I want to be? Then reach for its feeling, its spiritual sensation. What is that? I'll show you in a very simple way. Feel a piece of glass, now feel a baseball. Does the baseball feel like glass? Can you feel a tennis ball? Does it feel like a baseball or a piece of glass? Can you feel a piece of cloth, a violet, a piano? Do they all feel alike? Of course not. That's spiritual sensation . . a vivid way of seeing, hearing, smelling, tasting, and feeling reality.

604.   My brother Victor wanted to be a successful business man, and heknew how to remain faithful to what he imagined. In 1924, when our family didn't have a cent, Victor rearranged the name on a building (in his mind's eye) to imply we owned it. This he did for two years, when . . without any more money than when he started imagining . . a casual acquaintance purchased the building for us without collateral for $50,000. Eight years ago we sold the building to a bank for $850,000, and there is no capital gains tax in Barbados! Walking by faith, every day as Victor passed that building, he saw "J. C. Goddard and Sons" on the marquee in place of the existing name of "I. N. Roach & Company". Sight told him the building belonged to another, but faith said the building was his. By simply rearranging the structure of his mind every day for two years, our family's fortune changed. Now, we are told: "Faith is the assurance of things hoped for; the conviction of things not seen, so that what is seen was made out of things that do not appear." (Hebrews 11) Only my brother Victor saw his mental act. Others saw the sign, "J. N. Roach & Company" . . by sight, but Victor saw the words, "J.C. Goddard & Sons" . . by faith.

605.   Many times I have heard someone say: "I believe that imaginingcreates reality, but I once imagined something and it never came to pass." Then I ask: "What are you doing, saying: 'I once imagined it' and not imagining it now?' For God's name is I AM, not I did!" Always thinking of God as someone outside of himself, man finds it difficult to keep the tense, but God is the human imagination and there is no other God. When you imagine

you may include others, but do not think in terms of influence. Rather, think only in terms of clarity of form. Perhaps a friend would like a better job, more money, and greater responsibility. Before you imagine, take a moment and clarify the form your imaginal act will take. Are you giving the celebration party or is he? Who will be there? Fill the room with those who would want to share in the celebration. Raise your glass and say: "Here's to your fabulous new job, your salary increase, and the challenge of your greater responsibility!" Don't think in terms of trying to influence the friend's boss, for he could die or be discharged. Just go to the end. Toast the event, and do not think of influencing others.

The law, to be effective, needs feeling with form. Build a structure that would imply your desire is already fulfilled, and enter its form with feeling. You do not have to be concerned about influencing others, as they are not the cause . . your imaginal act is! Those who have a billion dollars are not causing your world. You and you alone are doing it, as your imaginal acts influence people. Everyone is yourself pushed out, so when you imagine, you are influencing yourself!

606.   Reality is controlled by feeling, as told us in the 27th chapter ofGenesis. The central character in this chapter is the state called Isaac, who has two sons . . Esau and Jacob. Esau is clothed in objective reality, while Jacob wears subjective reality as longings, wishes, and desires. When Jacob disguised himself as an objective fact, Isaac said: "Come near that I may feel you to determine whether you are Esau or not." And when he asked: "Are you really Esau?" Jacob answered, "I AM." Put yourself into a subjective state. Then feel the objectivity of the state by giving it sensory vividness and tones of reality. Then deceive yourself into believing that the image into which you have entered is now objectively real. Do that, and you have entered the state called Isaac. And we are told that when Isaac once more saw his objective world, Esau returned and Jacob disappeared. Then he realized that he had been self-deceived, but could not take back the blessing given to the subjective state. Although your objective world denies the reality of what you have done in your imagination, that which you have subjectively assumed is on its way to supplant your objective world and become your Esau.

You see, in life you are playing the part of Isaac with your two sons: Esau .
. your objective world, and Jacob . . your subjective one. Your subjective world
may seem to be clothed in unreality; but when you enter into its image in your
imagination and clothe that image with feeling, your subjective desire takes
on the tones of reality. This is how I do it: When I close my eyes this world is
shut out and I, like Isaac, am blind to the outer world. Then I feel myself into
the state of my desire. With my inner eye I see it all around me. I sense its
solidity, and when my five senses are awakened I have the feeling of relief,
knowing it is accomplished. When I open my physical eyes, Esau . . my physical
world . . returns and tries to persuade me that what I did was unreal. But
having done it time and time again, I know that my desire is moving towards
its objective fulfillment.

607.   A seamstress and dress designer I know wanted more money.
Usingher imagination, she held an envelope in her hand and listened to the
paper tear as she opened it. Shaking the contents out, she counted the money
to the very penny. This she did for seven nights. On the eighth day, a lady
called, offering her a job which paid her, to the penny, what she had imagined.
Do you know . . that lady could have counted out much more and she would
have received it, but she was quite satisfied with the amount she had
imagined. Now, if there is evidence for a thing, does it matter what the world
thinks? Could you ever take this lady's experience from her? No! The truth,
experienced by her parallels scripture, for all things are possible to one who
believes. How did this lady believe what she was imagining? She did it by
bringing forth all of her senses to bear upon this event. Using her sense of
hearing, she heard the paper tear. Shaking the contents of the envelope, she
heard the money fall on the table. She felt the envelope and saw the bills
inside. Do you know, money has an odor unlike anything else? So you can
smell money. She determined what she would do if she had the money and
she did it.

608.   I ask you to test your imagination! Go all out and believe in
whatyou have imagined. Do not try to influence anyone. Instead, put all of
your energies into clarity of form. If a certain desk designates that you are
occupying a desired position, occupy that desk. Enter into the image, and you
will realize your vision. Sit in the chair behind that desk and view the room.
Persist in thinking from that point of view. If you do not physically occupy that

chair tomorrow, and begin to doubt, ask yourself: "What am I doing, remembering and not imagining?" Then return to your chair behind that desk!

609.   Now we are told by the great Blake: "The spirit of Jesus is continualforgiveness of sin" . . forgiveness of sin every moment of time. Tonight when we go into the silence we can sit here for a minute and forgive each other. Suppose I could hear everyone here rise and tell the most fantastic story in the world about themselves or a friend, or a relative . . or someone. Suppose I, really wanting it to be told from this platform, sit in the silence and listen to that and that only . . the most fantastic story in the world that you could tell me individually. If I walk out of here tonight convinced that I heard it and remain loyal to what I have imagined I heard, I must hear it . . no power can stop it, if I remain loyal. If anyone says it has not worked, I am not asking any questions, but as far as I am concerned, it has worked. I am sure when I know the vision I am holding for you "has its own appointed hour, it will ripen and it will flower. If it seems long in coming, wait. It is sure, it will not be late." If I actually assume things are as I would like them to be of every being here, and I remain loyal, I either know the story is true or it is false. I know it is true. It can't fail. There is no power in the world to make it fail.

610.   If you do not believe you are this fabulous being, that your ownwonderful human imagination is the cause of the phenomena of your life, you are still searching for its cause. But when you are convinced, you will begin to awaken and discover that there never was another God. Then you will see how practical this vision of God really is. Your own wonderful human imagination is the Lord Jesus. Prove it! Believe in the only Jesus, for all things are made by him and without him is not anything made that is made. It is he who made the statement in the Book of Deuteronomy: "I kill and I make alive; I wound and I heal." The same being who wounds, heals, because imagination does it all! So you see how practical and wonderful this whole principle is? Tonight, if you really want something . . I don't care what it is . . you can have it. For your own sake I hope it will not injure another. You don't have to hurt anyone to get what you want; all you have to do is accept it! To live as though you had it now! And when you get it (and you will) I urge you to share your good news with others to encourage all.

611.   No one is without sin. At some time everyone has mentally coveted

or stolen. Describe a man in unflattering terms and you have stolen his good name. Everyone is guilty; therefore, do not analyze yourself, for if you do, you will miss your mark. To worry about what you may have done, is to waste your creative power. You will reap the tares as well as the wheat, as every imaginal act fulfills itself. But start now to plant something lovely . . not only for yourself, but for your neighbor, friend, or child. Fall in love with the idea that he is happy and secure. Feel the satisfaction that comes when one recognizes his harvest, for if a harvest is not recognized, there is no satisfaction. But when you do something consciously and see your harvest, you will receive enormous satisfaction. Prove your thoughts have creative power by consciously imaging constantly, and walk on the water. No matter what happens in the course of a day, revise it. Make the day conform to what you want it to be, and you are walking on the water.

612.   I tell you: everything is possible to the individual when he knowswho he is. You are the Joshua of the Old Testament and the Jesus of the New. And Jesus, your own wonderful human imagination, is Jehovah. He is your awareness, but as long as you see Jehovah as someone other than yourself you will not apply this principle. You must be willing to give up all foreign gods, all idols, and return to the one and only God, whose name is in you as your very being! If you were trained in the Christian faith, you were taught to believe that Jesus was on the outside. But how can you put him to the test if he is another? There never was another Joshua or Jehovah. There is only God, the director of the great dance of life whose dancers are himself. God plays the part of the bum and dances the dance of poverty. He also plays the part of a millionaire and dances to the tune of millions, as every part is being played by God. Now, everyone must act from where he is! Ask yourself: where am I? If I AM God, where can I go and God is not? If I make my bed in hell, God is there. If I make it in heaven, God is there, for everything penetrates me! I do not have to physically move. Simply by adjusting my thinking I can move from one state to another.

613.   If I desire to visit my island home in Barbados, but do not have themeans or the time to go there, I can enter its image in my imagination by

approaching it on the fiery chariot of my contemplative thought. I have done it. I do not use this wonder working power lightly anymore, because I know that after imagining, my desire fulfilled (although I may forget it) I will be compelled to experience it in this world of shadows. This wonder working power is to be used for anything you desire. It now penetrates your brain, and it is wherever you are. I know that Barbados is in the outer world, but I also know that I am all imagination. I know that God is Man and exists in us and we in Him; that the eternal body of Man is the Imagination, and that is God Himself. So if I . . imagination . . enter into an image I desire to occupy, no earthly power can stop that image from becoming an objective fact. What is the secret that makes this wonder working power operate? Feeling!

614.   Practice the art of imagining, and you will discover you can goanywhere and enter any time without the aid of anyone. Move in your imagination, and people will respond because of your action. Dare to assume you are wealthy, and watch everyone play their parts to provide you with the wealth you claim to have. They will, for they are only yourself pushed out. The world goes on and on, as the actors . . playing their numberless parts . . desire more and more things that vanish. Man is forever fighting for something that passes away; yet he is told: "Do not lay up treasures on earth where thieves can take and the moth corrupt, but lay up treasures in heaven where no man can take from you." The treasures of earth can be withdrawn at any moment, but the treasures in the instructions I am giving you now are forever.

615.   Are you willing to become enamored over a desire that much? Areyou willing to fall in love with its fulfillment that you imagine it is yours now? If so, I promise you it will out picture itself in your world. And when it does, you will have found Christ, for the words of scripture: "By him all things are made and without him is not anything made that is made," are false. When you test your imagination you will find He who produced your desire and the Maker of all things! I have tested him numberless times. I have taught this principle to others who have tested him and shared their experiences with me. Now I know who Jesus Christ really is. The words, "Unless you believe that I AM He, you will die in your sins," are not spoken on the outside, but on the inside. Now wearing a garment of flesh, my words appear to be coming from without, and one day I will seem to die and become a historical fact. But I am not speaking as an outer man. I am speaking as the true   Jesus

Christ, who comes in every individual by unfolding his story as recorded in scripture. There is only one story, and only one being to play the part. That being is God. It is he alone who acts and is in all things.

616.	Paul found Christ to be his human imagination and urged everyoneto test himself. Like Paul, I urge you to test your human imagination. You do not need the money or the time to go anywhere in your imagination, yet you can put yourself there, just as though you had made the trip. If you do, and your circumstances change so that the money and the time appears, allowing you to go, have you not found Jesus Christ to be your imagination? This is what scripture teaches, but man has personified the story and made Jesus Christ into a little idol to bow before, when the true God is the human imagination. All things are made by the human imagination. Imagine something that is not now a fact. Persist in your imaginal act, and when it becomes a fact, you have found God. And once you have found him, never let him go!

617.	When you truly believe that imagining creates reality, you will knowthere is no fiction. How can there be fiction when imagining is forever creating its reality? You may hear something you do not like, but because imagining creates reality what you heard was first imagined, or it could not have happened. When you revise the hearing by stopping the action and rewriting the script you are walking on the water, imagining the reality you desire to hear and appear in your world.

618.	At the end of the drama it is said that one who knew Jesus betrayedhim. Now, in order to betray someone, you must know his secret! So the one who knows the secret betrays him. That one is self! God is self-revealed. Unless God reveals himself to you, how will you ever know him? Turning to those who did not know him, Jesus said: "Now that you have found me, do not let me go, but let all these go." Let every belief of a power on the outside go, but do not let the belief in your powerful imagination go . . for truth is within you. When you find the Maker in yourself, then no matter what arguments the priesthoods may give, do not believe them, for the Christ you seek is the human imagination.

619.   When you imagine a state, do you believe that the scene has thepower to externalize itself? Or do you feel you must pray to a being on the outside for help? I tell you: there is no being on the outside. The creative power of the world is housed within you now. Sit down and imagine a state of confidence that it must externalize itself. Believe that because all things are possible to imagine, the state you have imagined must become an external fact. I have tried this time and time again, and it has always proved itself in performance. Now I share this knowledge with everyone who will listen. How many believe my words and put them into practice I do not know. I only know that man finds it hard to keep the tense. Religious leaders speak of God in the third person as if he were on the outside, yet I tell you he comes from within. When Moses heard the words: "I AM has sent me unto you," it seemed to come from without, yet it was whispered from within.

620.   "God actually became as we are, that we maybe as He is." [Blake,from "There Is No Natural Religion"] So when you imagine something, remember: It is God Acting! And God's actions are His words. "And His word cannot return unto Him void but it must accomplish that which He purposed, and prosper in the thing for which He sent it." Well, what are you imagining? Whatever you are imagining, you are actually sending into being to be confronted with it. So if you really want a lovely life, be careful what you are imagining, because imagination is God. Imagining is Godinaction! So what are you imagining? That everything is going down? That the whole world is collapsing? Well then, if that is what you imagine, may I tell you? You will have the experience of a collapsed world, but others won't.

621.   If God is in you, is there any place where God is not? And if there isno place where imagination is not, where would you go to be where you want to be? If everything penetrates you, then you must choose what you want and adjust yourself into the feeling that you are already there. You will know you have arrived when you view the world from there. Motion can be detected only by a change of position relative to another object. While physically sitting in a chair you appear not to move, but because everything penetrates you, by a mental adjustment you can think from the awareness of being the person you want to be. How will you know you have changed? By the expression on the faces of your friends. If they now see the new you, then

you have moved. So let them look at you until their faces tell you they are seeing that which you are assuming is true.

622.   All things are made by your imagination, for without imagining,nothing is made. Imagination is not limited to this level of consciousness. There are levels and levels of imagination, as your dreams and visions prove. This world is sustained by Divine Imagining, which is human imagining on a higher level. Our imagination is keyed low, but we are called upon to exercise this power, to examine ourselves to see if we are keeping our faith. On this level, faith is not complete until, through experiment, it becomes experience.

Experiment with this statement: "Whatever you desire, believe you have received it and you will." If faith is not complete until, through experiment it becomes experience, you must take an unseen objective and place it in an assemblage of mental states which would imply its fulfillment. Then this desire must be activated by entering into its center, feeling its reality, and walking in the faith that it will happen. I tell you: in a way you could not devise, what you have assumed will come into your world. You do not have to construct a bridge of incident to walk across; you simply move toward the fulfillment of what you have already prepared for yourself. Then fulfill another desire the same way, and when it appears you will know exactly what to do when confronted with any problem. You will simply turn your back upon it by constructing an imaginal scene which would imply the fulfillment of its solution. Activate it and let it come into being.

623.   I tell you: God became you, with all of your weakness andlimitations, that you may become Imagination. Becoming our imagination, God exists in us and we in him. Our eternal body is the imagination, and that is God Himself. And God alone acts! He can act the part of the fool, or the king, the poor, or the rich man. Every desire is a state. Move into your desire, and God will play that part . . as you! If you desire riches, yet do not know this power, you will remain poor because you are looking for a God on the outside, trying to coerce him into giving you wealth for acquiring merit. You can spend your life acquiring merit and be so good the world will think you are wonderful, yet remain poor. Man must seek and find his true

identity within himself, for he and he alone is the revealer and maker of everything in this world.

624.   Knowing what you want, assume your desire is already fulfilled byimagining a circle of friends are congratulating you. Fall asleep knowing that those who would empathize with you have already witnessed your good fortune. Knowing you have put the fulfillment of your desire in motion, walk confident that what you are assuming is true. And when it happens, share your experience with others, in the hope that they will try it and it will work for them. It does not matter to me what others think, for I have found my Father . . the one the world worships and calls God . . to be my own wonderful human imagination!

6\25. So, I only ask you to be as faithful to any imaginal state in this world, no matter what it is. In everyone God resides. Everyone has to say, "I AM." That is God. I AM Einstein, I AM Neville. I AM is God. Neville is a tiny thing resting on the foundation that is God. I AM rich . . that is a tiny thing on the foundation of God, and God is Infinity, God is Everything. Therefore, whatever you say, before you say it, you say, "I AM".

626. I urge you to use your imagination for everything that is lovely andloving. I don't care what your desire may be . . your imagination will give it to you, for the human imagination is the divine body the world calls Jesus. Because you can imagine and I can imagine, we are members of that one divine body, and all things are possible to him. There is not a thing impossible to God. All you need do is imagine its fulfillment! Faith is an experiment which ends as an experience. Experiment by believing you already have all that you desire, and you will have the experience.

627. Christ is your own wonderful human imagination. That's an awfulshock, and when you first hear it your world collapses, for there is no one to turn to but self! Formerly you could point to another as the cause of your misfortune, but you can no longer do that when you discover who Jesus Christ really is. From that moment on you must turn to yourself to blame or praise. And when you have played all of the parts, you will find him of whom you seek, Jesus of Nazareth!

628. A thought acted upon is an imaginal act. Think (imagine) a horribleearthquake and God will give it to you. Imagine (think of) a war and God will provide that, too. Imagine peace and you will have it. God will give you health if you will but imagine being healthy. Imagine success and you will have it. The moment you think, you are feeding your imagination, which is a person. I use the word person deliberately, for you are a person. You are the mask God is now wearing, for God became you that you may become God.

629.*"He was in the world, and the world was made by Him and the world knew Him not. The mystery hid from the ages; Christ in you, the hope of glory."*

The "He" in the first of these quotations is your imagination. As previously explained, there is only one substance. This substance is consciousness. It is your imagination which forms this substance into concepts, which concepts are then manifested as conditions, circumstances, and physical objects. Thus imagination made your world. This supreme truth, with but few exceptions, man is not conscious of. The mystery, *"Christ in you"*,referred to in the second quotation, is your imagination, by which your world is molded. The hope of glory is your awareness of the ability to rise perpetually to higher levels. Christ is not to be found in history, nor in external forms. You find Christ only when you become aware of the fact that your imagination is the only redemptive power. When this is discovered, the "towers of dogma will have heard the trumpets of Truth, and, like the walls of Jericho, crumble to dust".

630.   *"Now unto Him that is able to do exceeding abundantly above all that we ask or think, according to the power that worketh in us, unto Him be glory."*

Him, that is able to do more than you can ask or think, is your imagination, and the power that worketh in us is your attention. Understanding imagination to be him that is able to do all that you ask, and attention to be the power by which you create your world, you can now build your ideal world. Imagine yourself to be the ideal you dream of and desire. Remain attentive to this imagined state, and as fast as you completely feel that you are already this ideal it will manifest itself as reality in your world.

631.   "The mystery hid from the ages... Christ in you, the hope of glory,"isyour imagination. This is the mystery which I am ever striving to realize more keenly myself and to urge upon others. Imagination is our redeemer, "the Lord from Heaven"

632.   Imagination's birth and growth is the gradual transition from a Godof tradition to a God of experience. If the birth of Christ (imagination) in man seems slow, it is only because man is unwilling to let go the comfortable but false anchorage of tradition. When imagination is discovered as the first principle of religion, the stone of literal understanding will have felt the rod of Moses and, like the rock of Zin, issue forth the water of psychological meaning to quench the thirst of humanity; and all who take the proffered cup and live a life according to this truth will transform the water of psychological meaning into the wine of forgiveness. Then, like the good Samaritan, they will pour it on the wounds of all. The Son of God is not to be found in history, nor in any external form. He can only be found as the imagination of him in whom His presence becomes manifest.

633.   Truth depends upon the intensity of the imagination, not uponexternal facts. Facts are the fruit bearing witness of the use or misuse of the imagination. Truth cannot be encompassed by facts. As we awaken to the imaginative life, we discover that to imagine a thing is to make it so, that a true judgment need not conform to the external reality to which it relates. The imaginative man does not deny the reality of the sensuous outer world of Becoming, but he knows that it is the inner world of continuous Imagination that is the force by which the sensuous outer world of Becoming is brought to pass. He sees the outer world and all its happenings as projections of the inner world of Imagination. To him, everything is a manifestation of the mental activity which goes on in man's imagination, without the sensuous reasonable man being aware of it. But he realizes that every man must become conscious of this inner activity and see the relationship between the inner causal world of imagination and the sensuous outer world of effects. It is a marvelous thing to find that you can imagine yourself into the state of your fulfilled desire and escape from the jails which ignorance built. The Real Man is a Magnificent Imagination. It is this self that must be awakened.

634.   The moment man discovers that his imagination is Christ, heaccomplishes acts which on this level can only be called miraculous. But until man has the sense of Christ as his imagination, "You did not choose me, I have chosen you." He will see everything in pure objectivity without any subjective relationship. Not realizing that all that he encounters is part of himself, he rebels at the thought that he has chosen the conditions of his life, that they are related by affinity to his own mental activity. Man must firmly come to believe that reality lies within him and not without. Although others have bodies, a life of their own, their reality is rooted in you, ends in you, as yours ends in God.

635.   I was first made conscious of the power, nature, and redemptivefunction of imagination through the teachings of my friend Abdullah; and through subsequent experiences, I learned that Jesus was a symbol of the coming of imagination to man, that the test of His birth in man was the individual's ability to forgive sin; that is, his ability to identify himself or another with his aim in life. Without the identification of man with his aim, the forgiveness of sin is an impossibility, and only the Son of God can forgive sin. Therefore, man's ability to identify himself with his aim, though reason and his senses deny it, is proof of the birth of Christ in him. To passively surrender to appearances and bow before the evidence of facts is to confess that Christ is not yet born in you.

636.   "You must imagine yourself right into the state of your fulfilleddesire", Abdullah told me. The world which we describe from observation must be as we describe it relative to ourselves. Our imagination connects us with the state desired. But we must use imagination masterfully, not as an onlooker thinking of the end, but as a partaker thinking from the end. We must actually be there in imagination. If we do this, our subjective experience will be realized objectively. "This is not mere fancy", said he, "but a truth you can prove by experience." His appeal to enter into the wish fulfilled was the secret of thinking from the end. Every state is already there as "mere possibility" as long as you think of it, but is overpoweringly real when you think from it. Thinking from the end is the way of Christ.

637."Does a firm persuasion that a thing is so, make it so?" And the prophet replied, "All poets believe that it does. And in ages of imagination, this firm persuasion removed mountains: but many are not capable of a firm persuasion of anything." . . . Blake *"Let every man be fully persuaded in his own mind."*Persuasion is an inner effort of intense attention. To listen attentively as though you heard is to evoke, to activate. By listening, you can hear what you want to hear and persuade those beyond the range of the outer ear. Speak it inwardly in your imagination only. Make your inner conversation match your fulfilled desire. What you desire to hear without, you must hear within. Embrace the without within and become one who hears only that which implies the fulfillment of his desire, and all the external happenings in the world will become a bridge leading to the objective realization of your desire.

638. To change your life, you must change your inner talking, for "life",said Hermes, "is the union of Word and Mind". When imagination matches your inner speech to fulfilled desire, there will then be a straight path in yourself from within out, and the without will instantly reflect the within for you, and you will know reality is only actualized inner talking.

639. Man's ignorance of the future is the result of his ignorance of hisinner talking. His inner talking mirrors his imagination, and his imagination is a government in which the opposition never comes into power. If the reader asks, "What if the inner speech remains subjective and is unable to find an object for its love?", the answer is: it will not remain subjective, for the very simple reason that inner speech is always objectifying itself.

640. The Real Man, the Imaginative Man, has invested the outer worldwith all of its properties. The apparent reality of the outer world which is so hard to dissolve is only proof of the absolute reality of the inner world of his own imagination. "No man can come to me, except the Father which hath sent me draw him... I and My Father are One." The world which is described from observation is a manifestation of the mental activity of the observer.

When man discovers that his world is his own mental activity made visible, that no man can come unto him except he draws him, and that there is no one to change but himself, his own imaginative self, his first impulse is to reshape the world in the image of his ideal. But his ideal is not so easily incarnated. In that moment when he ceases to conform to external discipline, he must impose upon himself a far more rigorous discipline, the selfdiscipline upon which the realization of his ideal depends. Imagination is not entirely untrammeled and free to move at will without any rules to constrain it. In fact, the contrary is true.

Imagination travels according to habit. Imagination has choice, but it chooses according to habit. Awake or asleep, man's imagination is constrained to follow certain definite patterns. It is this benumbing influence of habit that man must change; if he does not, his dreams will fade under the paralysis of custom. Imagination, which is Christ in man, is not subject to the necessity to produce only that which is perfect and good. It exercises its absolute freedom from necessity by endowing the outer physical self with free will to choose to follow good or evil, order or disorder. "Choose this day whom ye will serve." But after the choice is made and accepted, so that it forms the individual's habitual consciousness, then imagination manifests its infinite power and wisdom by molding the outer sensuous world of becoming in the image of the habitual inner speech and actions of the individual.

641. Blessed are they whose imagination has been so purged of thebeliefs in second causes they know that imagination is all, and all is imagination.

THE
END